THE IMAGE OF THE JEW
IN FRENCH LITERATURE
FROM 1800 TO 1908

THE IMAGE OF THE JEW
IN FRENCH LITERATURE
FROM 1800 TO 1908

By
MOSES DEBRÉ

Translated by
GERTRUDE HIRSCHLER

Introduction by
ANNA KRAKOWSKI

KTAV PUBLISHING HOUSE, Inc.

NEW YORK

1970

SBN 87068-075-7

LIBRARY OF CONGRESS CATALOG CARD NUMBER: 79-106524
MANUFACTURED IN THE UNITED STATES OF AMERICA

TABLE OF CONTENTS

INTRODUCTION

Despite its modest appearance, Debré's study, so different from most modern literary criticism, is a work of unusual historical interest. It affords us a glimpse of the complex relationship between Frenchman and Jew as seen by a Jew of Alsace during the period prior to World War I, when that province was under German rule.

The Image of the Jew in French Literature from 1800 to 1908 was written at a critical juncture in the history of French Jewry, when the political upheavals that came in the wake of the notorious Dreyfus Affair brought the Jews of France face to face with a fact they initially refused to accept; that all of so-called modern civilization was only a veneer, a thin cover beneath which there still lay, intact, a mass of medieval ignorance and superstition.

The racial anti-Semitism of the 1880's, of which the Dreyfus Affair was a direct outgrowth, came as a surprise rather than as a shock to the Jews of France, convinced as they were that anti-Jewish prejudice was inconsistent with the basic principles and with the national genius of the country in which they lived. The liberal Catholic, Anatole Leroy-Beaulieu, too, viewed this new type of Jew-hatred as something un-French, a product of Teutonic arrogance and of the reactionary ideas of benighted Tsarist autocracy. Analyzing the anti-Semitism of his day, Leroy-Beaulieu discusses the various elements, old and new, that went into the making of this phenomenon—vestiges of medievalism, the instincts of reaction, the passions of the revolutionaries and, alas, illusory socialism as well.[1]

[1]Anatole Leroy-Beaulieu, *Israël Chez Les Nations*, Paris, Calmann-Lévy, 1893. *Préface*, p. iii.

1

Like Jew-haters throughout history, that breed of French politicians used an age-old prejudice as a convenient means of furthering their cause and attaining their ends. They tailored their arguments to the requirements of expediency, mob psychology, and the politization of the masses. By the second half of the nineteenth century politization had reached a point where the individual had abdicated his personal intellectual and moral responsibilities to the group with which he identified and which, in turn, acquitted itself of its burden by blaming all its troubles on others. As the smallest and weakest of all groups in France, the Jews became the chief victims of this new attitude.

The initial response of all but a very few Jews in France was to do nothing. Most French Jews considered it unnecessary to initiate action against what they regarded as no more than a temporary aberration. Besides, they feared that a strong reaction on their part might give undue importance and added impetus to the anti-Semitic movement.[2]

Even after the recrudescence of anti-Semitism had come to a head in the Dreyfus Affair, the Jews clung to their belief that "Liberty, Equality, Fraternity" was still the watchword of France. It seemed as if they deliberately shut their eyes to the avalanche of vicious anti-Semitic literature that swelled with each passing day. Absorbed by their desperate efforts to shake off the effect of the nightmare of the Dreyfus Affair, they seemed unaware that, beneath their eyes, the realization of the dream of two thousand years was taking shape that very moment on French soil. It appears strange to us today that the sequence of three historic developments— the rise of modern anti-Semitism, the Dreyfus Affair, and the birth of political Zionism—should have been lost upon the compatriots of the soldier who had been deported to Devil's Island to expiate the sin of having been born a Jew. The Jews of France strained to see the positive aspects of the tragic situation. Miscarriages of justice occurred all over the world, but where else except in France, they asserted, could

[2]The only prominent French Jews to react, after a fashion, were Chief Rabbi Zadoc Cahn and the Socialist leader, Bernard Lazare.

such an incident have split a whole country into two opposing camps in a struggle for right to prevail?

All these ideological stresses found expression in the French literature of the late nineteenth and early twentieth centuries. The works analyzed in Debré's study, and the writings of other French authors, faithfully reflect the hostilities as well as the sympathies of the French public of the time. As for Debré, cut off from France as he was through the German occupation of his native province, his view of the mentality and the sensitivities of French Jews and of their reaction to contemporary literature dealing with their political and social problems is of necessity colored by nostalgia. In his study, he harks back to the great days of the French Revolution of 1789. Dwelling in detail on the radical changes the Revolution had wrought in the position of French Jewry, Debré attempts to show how these changes were reflected in French literature. In his eyes, the Jew in nineteenth-century French literature is no longer a type apart. Regardless of the light in which he may be portrayed, his image does not correspond to that conveyed by authors of bygone centuries.

It must be pointed out that Debré's interpretation represents a slight exaggeration of fact. Even aside from the French theatre of the nineteenth century, where Jewish characters were still shown as odious and grotesque, we find the conventional "Jewish" stereotypes still very much alive also in the works of Romantics such as Victor Hugo and George Sand.

Adolphe d'Ennery, a French playwright of Jewish origin, has the following explanation for the absence of Jewish characters in his works:

> The reason [for their absence] is very simple. I believe that in the theater one should not fly in the face of public sentiment. The first duty of an author is to please his audiences; that is, to respect their tastes and habits. Were I to present a Jew, then, I naturally would have had to make him a usurer, a scoundrel or a traitor . . . in any case, he would have to be an evil character. That would have been un-

pleasant, for I myself am of Jewish origin. What did I do, therefore? I have simply passed over the Jews. You will not find a single Jew in any of my plays. Instead, you will meet plenty of Catholic missionaries who throw themselves into the flames to save children in peril, and if I have not completely invented this sort of martydom, I have certainly played it for all it is worth.[3]

No less an author than Alexandre Dumas the Younger pointed out in his preface to *La Femme de Claude*: "It is taken for granted that the Jewish character in drama must be portrayed as a grotesque figure."

If the author of *The Image of the Jew in French Literature from 1800 to 1908* alludes to this tendency only in passing, Abraham Dreyfus[4] dwells at some length on the image of the Jew presented in the theater of his day. Dreyfus does not consider the unfavorable portrayal of the Jew on the French stage as reflecting hostility or an intent to downgrade the Jew. He sees it merely as a literary habit of yesteryear, retained to cater to the tastes of French theatergoers. It pleased French audiences to ridicule the Jews or to see them held up to ridicule. Dreyfus has no objections as long as French playwrights followed this practice in their portrayal of Jews of an earlier age. However, he strongly feels that it should not be indulged in to the detriment of the French Jew of modern times:

> That the Jew[ish stereotype] should continue to be presented in the theater as a character of times past, and that as a character in a more or less historical drama, he should be burdened with all the shortcomings of the people of Israel—to this I see no objection.
> But in our own modern theatre . . . to have Jewish characters acting as Jews seems to me as wrong and as outdated as it would be to have a Breton character representing all the home virtues simply because he is a Breton.[5]

[3]Abraham Dreyfus, "Le Juif au Théatre," *Revue des Études Juives*, 1886, p. 52.
[4]French playwright active at the end of the nineteenth century.
[5]Abraham Dreyfus, *op.cit.*, p. 62.

The Dreyfus logic seems a little weak. However, it can be explained in terms of two basic interrelated tendencies: unwillingness on his part to identify with the past and his conviction that the French Jew has attained the exalted status of "Frenchman of the Jewish faith."

Debré does not devote as much space to anti-Semitic literature as he does to what he calls "philo-Semitic" writings. Thus, he fails to mention such authors as Vigneaux, Simond, Ohnet, Orcet and Chercusac, all of whom were well-known during the second half of the nineteenth century. He says nothing at all about the work of Paul Adam, and very little about that of Gyp (Sibylle Martel de Janville, Comtesse de Mirabeau), which compensates for its lack of literary merit by its virulent anti-Semitism and ingenuity in devising grotesque and demeaning names for Jewish characters. In his discussion of the Goncourt brothers and Alphonse Daudet, Debré mentions neither the anti-Semitic remarks in the Goncourts' *Journal*[6] nor Daudet's anti-Jewish prejudices and the support he gave Edouard Drumont when the latter published *La France Juive*.[7] Although Debré includes in his study Sephora from Daudet's *Les Rois en Exil* (The Kings in Exile) as one of the most repulsive female characters in all of literature, he does not place sufficient stress on the fact that she was intended to portray the typical Jewess as seen by the anti-Semites of the day—the grasping usurer.

Debré takes great pains to stress the transformation which, he asserts, the Jewish money-lender is supposed to have undergone in nineteenth-century French literature. The sordid and contemptible usurer of older French writings, he points out, has yielded place to the mighty banker to whom all the powers that be must bow.

[6]Published between 1888 and 1896.

[7]Mme. A. Daudet, *Souvenirs autour d'un groupe littéraire*.

J. P. Sartre describes Drumont's *La France Juive* as a "collection of base and obscene stories." Because Drumont take a perverse pleasure in evil, Sartre says, he (Drumont) "is able to repeat to the point of obsession the recital of obscene and criminal acts which stimulate and satisfy his own perverse inclinations, but he attributes them to the infamous Jews whom he attacks and despises. In this manner he gratifies his urges without compromising his own good name." (J. P. Sartre, *La Question Juive*, Gallimard, Paris, 1954, pp. 54-55).

Here, again, there is room for disagreement. The fact is that the vice of usury is very apparent even in the modern-day bankers who appear in French literature of the 1800's and early 1900's. In the anti-Semitic literature, and even in the so-called "neutral" literary products of nineteenth-century France, the Jewish banker has gained neither respectability nor moral rehabilitation. One needs only to study the works of the many writers who make up for their lack of talent with generous doses of malice, and who make the Jewish banker of their day no better than the usurers of centuries past. The Jewish characters presented by Charnaice, Roustane,[8] Maizeroy and Bonnières concentrate in their persons all the vices that can possibly be associated with usurers, parvenus and other scum. They are grotesque and obnoxious Jewish stereotypes.

The Jewish banker featured in nineteenth-century French literature stands out for his lack of human dignity and conscience. That this mythical image of the Jew was accepted even by some enlightened and broad-minded individuals is shown by the fact that Leroy-Beaulieu, attempting to defend the Jews, feels called upon to make excuses for the absense of these two virtues in Jews. Where, he asks, could the Jews have had a chance to acquire a sense of honor and dignity? "Feudal man, in his dungeon, had to have pride if he was to survive. The Jew, by contrast, had to make himself humble and small if he wanted to go on living. That was the price he had to pay for his survival."[9]

Naturally, it all depends on what we understand by human dignity and conscience, and it is reasonable to assume that even some of the best-intentioned minds have not yet entirely shaken off the vestige influences of the Middle Ages. The fact is that the Jew has never allowed himself to be drowned by the deluge of contempt that threatened to overwhelm him. Despite all conceivable odds the Jew of old strove to survive the cruelty of his foes for the sake of an ideal of

[8] Roustane justifies a pogrom in Russia by explaining it as nothing but a reaction to Jewish usury at its worst.

[9] Leroy-Beaulieu, *op.cit.*, pp. 226–231.

the future, toward which he was advancing with much firmer strides than his emancipated descendants of a later age.

Notwithstanding his talent, which was widely admired in his day, Paul Bourget never succeeded in putting aside his anti-Jewish prejudices in his work. Accordingly, he views the financier Justus Hafner, the Jewish character of his *Cosmopolis*, in a perspective that might have been more readily expected in Bourget's less talented literary predecessors of whom mentioned has already been made. Bourget in this case does not behave as a psychologist but merely as a mediocre cataloguer of "Jewish" shortcomings which, when present and prominent in one single individual of consequence, can lead to the moral decline of an entire country, in this case France. Not so Honoré Balzac who, despite his frank hostility toward the Jews, is able to depart from conventional Jewish stereotypes in his writings because the literary talent of Balzac the author is greater than his personal prejudices. Balzac's Gobsec is a puzzling figure, a strange combination of philosopher and usurer—a unique example of two souls dwelling in one body. Even if we are led to suspect that the philosopher in Gobsec derives from his Dutch background while the usurer in him is a throwback to his Jewish antecedents, his character as such is a work of literary art which makes the reader forget the original intentions of Balzac the man.

As for the hero of *La Maison Nucingen*, Balzac admits that Nucingen is a genius, and admires him for it. However, he does not make of him the "Jewish" type he probably intended to portray. Ingrained dishonesty masquerading as honesty is not a trait typical of Jews. Nucingen's married life, too, is not typically Jewish by any stretch of the imagination. Furthermore, it seems a little unrealistic that, given the rather hostile non-Jewish environment in which he lived, Nucingen should have been able to pass as an honest man in the eyes of his public.

Along with Nucingen, nineteenth-century French literature features a more complex and more widely-studied banker type, portrayed against the background of the great and mysterious Stock Exchange. Emile Zola's *ébauche*[10] of *L'Argent* contains some uncomplimentary insinuations about Jews, which are open to debate, but it should be noted at the outset that Zola consistently tries to be objective.

He constantly checks the veracity of his sources of information and does not ever allow himself to be led to the wrong conclusions. Here, plain for all to see, is the strength of the searcher for truth. In *L'Argent,* Zola presents a confrontation between two opposing concepts—high finance, which is represented by Gundermann, and the modern school of banking, personified by Saccard. He shows a clear insight into two basic difference between the two: the hard-hearted Jewish financier, descended from a long line of bankers, backed by "old money," and interested solely in amassing as huge a fortune as possible, speculates only with his own capital, while his Gentile adversary, extravagant and hot-headed, gambles only with the wealth of others. The two characters are based on actual figures prominent in the history of French finance. Gundermann is meant to represent Baron James de Rothschild; Saccard is the counterpart of Bontoux, the driving force behind the Union Générale, a banking enterprise owned by French Catholics. Zola does not limit his effort to character sketching, but seeks to explore in depth one of the fundamental problems exploited by anti-Semitic propaganda. Zola's merit is that he has tried to explain the problem and to present it in its proper perspective.

The plot of *L'Argent* is based on the conflict which took place between the Union Générale and the Rothschild bank. Bontoux had enlisted the help of the Austrian statesman Count Taafe, a notorious anti-Semite, in depriving the Jewish bankers of the *de facto* monopoly they had held until that time on Austrian loans and major railway transactions. When the Catholic bank failed as a result of some unwise speculations, anti-Semitic circles were quick to blame the disaster on the machinations of a syndicate of "operators" supposedly master-minded by the Rothschilds.

[10]Author's first rough outline of a projected novel, including pertinent observations, documented information and research notes.

Zola's plot is the reverse of the story of Balzac's *House of Nucingen*. In *L'Argent* a Gentile employed by a Jewish banker steals a brainstorm from his employer which enables him to set up his own banking concern and, before long, to outdistance the Jew on the way to financial power. The information Zola had gathered from such friends as Fasquelle, Busnach and Du Camp to the effect that "the abstract aspects of financial operations are incompatible with the French mind," that "this sort of thing is a Jewish specialty" and that success in the world of finance requires a talent peculiar to the Jewish race[11] might have appeared quite plausible to Zola. After all, it was convincing and well-documented evidence.

Up to that point Zola had almost never dealt with Jewish problems[12] in his writings; it seems that he had had no clear-cut ideas on the subject. Since practically everybody, from the socialists to the reactionaries, was talking about international Jewish finance, the concept must have become quite plausible to Zola. He must certainly have known about Karl Marx's essay *Zur Judenfrage*[13] and the anti-Semitic writings of such French socialists as Toussenel[14] and Proudhon.[15]

The information he gathered about the operations of the Stock Exchange was of the sort to arouse the novelist's curiosity and to stimulate his imagination. He saw in it another

[11]Ms. *Nouvelles Acquisitions Françaises,* No. 10269, ff. 102–103.

[12]Those few Jewish characters which appear in his works subsequent to *L'Argent* are different from his Gentiles only in that they have "Jewish" names. Cf. M. Le Blond, "Les personnages juifs dans l'oeuvre d'Emile Zola" (Jewish Characters in the Writings of Emile Zola), in *Revue de Genève,* 1936, No. IV.

[13]Marx wrote *Zur Judenfrage* and became a socialist in the 1840's. The important role played by bankers like the Rothschilds in the affairs of conservative states and in the industrialization of Europe confirmed Marx in the opinion he had formed about the Jews, drawing his inspiration from Voltaire and Diderot. Moreover, his opinion of commercial capitalism further increased the antagonism he felt toward Jews.

[14]Alphonse Toussenel, *Les Juifs rois de l'époque* (The Jews, Kings of the Age), Paris, 1847.

[15]Henri Grégoire and H. C. Poinsot, *Le Centenaire de Proudhon* (The Centenary of Proudhon); J. Salvyn Shapiro, *Pierre J. Proudhon, Harbinger of Fascism.*

symbolic phenomenon reminiscent of *L'Assomoir,* of the locomotive in *La Bête Humaine* and of Paradou in *La Faute de l'Abbé Mouret,* and assiduously recorded in his notes what Du Camp had had to say on the subject: "The absolute mystery of this, the terrors and the charms of the unknown prospects of gain. . . ." He did not hesitate to add in his notes: "I must put this into my very first chapter. The Stock Exchange in the heart of Paris, like a mysterious and yawning cavern, where things happen that nobody understands."[16]

Despite every temptation to do so, Zola feels that he must not put blind trust in the information he has received from his friends or from books about the failure of the Union Générale. Instead, he prefers to gather his facts from a qualified individual, an attorney named Georges Lévy. Zola's notes on the information received from Lévy show that the lawyer has disabused the writer of earlier notions he may have had. "M. Lévy," Zola writes, "does not believe there is such a thing as a syndicate of operators or a [Jewish] conspiracy to depress stock values. According to him, developments at the Stock Exchange cannot be 'brought on' or predicted. One can take advantage of these developments only at the time they actually occur. This is tantamount to saying that the truth of the matter is that the Stock Exchange is a very powerful factor which comes out on top no matter what. Here, logic reigns supreme. In the final analysis, it is logic that counts. To win out at the crucial moment, it is enough to have logic on your side.[17] In his novel, Zola goes along with Lévy's view; he points out that Gundermann had not caused the crash but had merely taken advantage of it when it happened.[18] He supports his statement with evidence taken from the court files of the Bontoux-Feder case. There is no doubt but that it was Zola's aim to clear up a ticklish question which the anti-Semites of his day had exploited for their purposes.

[16]Ms. N.A.F. No. 10269, pp. 102–103. The works consulted by Zola include a number of frankly anti-Semitic writings such as *La Bourse* by Eugène Mirecourt.

[17]The mysterious aspect of the Stock Exchange is underlined also in his revised conception of the institution. Ms. 10269 f. 157.

[18]*Ibid.,* f. 166.

Zola has not had much contact with the Jews, but once he has the proper information, he acts in character and puts himself squarely on the side of justice. While he certainly does not regard the Jewish banker as his ideal, he comes down also on his detractors, the anti-Semites.

Massias, a minor employee in a stock-broker's office, rationlizes his failures with the dictum that you have to be Jewish to do well at the Stock Exchange. This excuse not only relieves him of any feelings of inadequacy he may have, but also heightens his sense of Gentile prestige. When he has a stroke of luck, he changes his tune; he no longer says that you have to be Jewish to do well, but he reverts to his old rationalization when he loses everything in the crash. The better to bring out the absurdity of Massias' excuse,[19] Zola names in his novel several Gentiles, such as Daigremont and the Marquis de Bohain, who are no less capable than the Jews when it comes to playing the Stock Exchange.

Zola makes a violent attack on anti-Semitism through his principal character, Saccard. Hot-headed and impervious to reason and experience, Saccard refuses to admit he has made a mistake and prefers to blame his troubles on a convenient scapegoat. "Oh, that Gundermann . . . it's all of Jewry, stubborn, cold, conquering, on the march to world rule among the peoples they have bought off, one by one, with almighty gold . . . one day, he'll be lord of the world. . . . Yes, that hatred for Jews, I've had it in my bones from way back; it's at the very root of my being."[20]

Linking his personal hostility with a general, quasi-eternal hatred, Saccard takes up Bontoux's diatribe: "The Universelle [Zola's substitute for the Union Générale]—strangled by the Government so that Gundermann can carry on his business! Any Catholic bank that gets too powerful is crushed, like a public enemy, to assure that ultimate triumph of the

[19]Sartre defines anti-Semitism as "an effort at giving status to mediocrity in order to create an elite of the mediocre. As far as the anti-Semite is concerned, intelligence is a Jewish trait and hence may be safely held in contempt like any of the other qualities the Jews possess" (*La Question Juive*, p. 27).

[20]*L'Argent*, pp. 413–414.

Jews who will eat us all alive, and soon."[21] Zola skillfully counters these accusations with the true reasons for the crash and demolishes all the arguments of Saccard which are those that were cited in real life by Bontoux and his defenders. Zola himself frequently speaks through Caroline Hamelin, who says: "To me, the Jews are people like anybody else. If they are different, it is because we have made them so."[22]

In the same vein Zola was to defend the Jews, in an article in *Le Figaro,* against Drumont's attacks.[23]

When Zola fights the Jewish bankers, he attacks them not as Jews but only as financiers who trample the poor underfoot. Even after he had sacrificed his whole life[24] and his honor for the Jewish cause, which he saw as the cause of justice, he continued to rake the Jewish capitalist over the coals. In *Vérité,* he describes his feelings at the sight of the castle owned by Nathan, a Jew who trades in gold: "An inextinguishable memory returned to Marc's mind,[25] that of the little dark shop [of Simon's parents-in-law] in the Rue du Trou. And all the other Jews, even worse off, who died of starvation in the filthy ratholes! These were the vast majority, and they expose the idiotic lie of anti-Semitism, that wholesale outlawing of an entire race, accusing it of seeking to monopolize the world's wealth when, in fact, there are among the Jews so many poor working people, so many victims of society, ground underfoot by the forces of money, Jewish and Catholic alike. As soon as a Jew becomes a captain of finance, he buys a title for himself, marries off his daughter to a count of old lineage, tries to act more royalist than the king himself and ends up as a renegade, a rabid anti-Semite, disowning his people and cutting their throats. There is no such thing as a Jewish problem; there is only the problem of money heaped, poisoned and corrupting."[26]

[21]*Ibid.,* p. 414.

[22]*Ibid.*

[23]*Le Figaro,* May 16, 1896.

[24]Reliable sources give us reason to assume that Zola's death was not accidental. It was murder, deliberately planned by his enemies.

[25]Marc is the author's mouthpiece.

[26]*Vérité,* p. 90.

The ideal character in *L'Argent* is a Jew whose goal is to abolish filthy lucre and to establish the reign of justice on earth. Sigismond Busch has all the virtues of the idealist and injects a Messianic and socialist note into this story of the all-powerful idol that is the Stock Exchange.[27] Leroy-Beau-lieu, who has little use for naturalists, cannot help expressing his approval of Zola's insight as shown by his realization that the money-man is not identical with all of Israel. "In *L'Argent*," he writes, "M. Zola, who on occasion plays at symbolism, presents as the counterfoil of the banker, the king of the stock exchange, a little consumptive Jew who, at death's door, cherishes visions of the regeneration of society. Sigismond is not a figment of Zola's imagination; I have known others like him."[28]

At that time Zola saw only one solution for the Jewish problem; namely, assimilation. In his reply to Drumont and the other anti-Semites, he writes that their strategy is wrong; instead of persecuting the Jews, they should do just the opposite. "Open your arms wide to them; turn the equality sanctioned by the *Code Napoléon* into social reality. Embrace the Jews so that we can absorb them, make them merge with us, and enrich ourselves with such good qualities as they have. Stop the struggle between the races by getting them to intermingle. Promote intermarriage and leave it to the offspring of these unions to reconcile their parents. This, and this alone, is the task of unification; herein, and herein only, lies the true achievement of human liberation."[29]

Zola considered this an adequate rebuttal of the views of the anti-Semites, who stressed the impossibility of assimilating the Jewish race, as does Donnay,[30] whose *Retour de Jérusalem* features a converted Jewess, who remains very much a Jewess and a stranger to the Gentile world. His

[27]Cf. M. Le Blond, "Les personnages juifs dans l'oeuvre d'Emile Zola," *Revue de Genève*, 1936, IV, p. 308.

[28]Leroy-Beaulieu, p. 333.

[29]*Le Figaro*, May 16, 1896.

[30]Donnay, who had been helped in his career as a playwright by Jewish friends, repays his debt to them by showing how the Jews force their way into a society with which they are unable to identify.

heroine, Judith de Chouzé, has character traits which the anti-Semites consider typically Jewish. Her egotism and her lack of consideration even for her lover are truly revolting. She can care only for Jews. It is surprising that Debré fails to bring out the fact that the clash between these two lovers is not typical of a "mixed" couple, and that Judith and her paramour simply are not true-to-life characters. Imagine a Jewish convert to Christianity who takes her Gentile lover on a honeymoon pilgrimage to Jerusalem, and to the Wailing Wall at that! It is difficult to conceive that a man like Michel, who has stoically endured this pilgrimage and the wailing Jews, should start rebelling against it all only after he has returned home to Paris. Once the couple is back in France, we learn that Michel cannot stand Judith's Jewish friends, and he tells us exactly what he thinks of the Jews, dwelling at length on the incompatibility between Jews and Aryans. In his eyes all the Jews who frequent Judith's salon are either avowed enemies of France or at least bad citizens and anti-militarists.

In the second section of his study, Debré cites numerous writers who do not share Donnay's views. Many non-Jewish writers, and some Jewish authors as well, follow the lead of Erckmann-Chatrian and portray the Jews of the Alsace and of France proper in quite apologetic terms. In these writings there is no conflict between Jew and Gentile. This gallery of characters, which should be of great interest to any student of that particular era in French history, requires no further comment.

Things get somewhat more complicated in the case of authors like Anatole France. Here we see how over-simplification can lead to error. It is obvious that Debré thoroughly approves of Worms-Clavelin,[31] the Jewish prefect in Anatole France's L'Orme du Mail. This high official enjoys universal popularity and esteem; he is liked and respected even by the Sisters at the convent where his daughter is being educated.

[31]Worms-Clavelin is one of the principal characters in a four-volume opus, L'Historie Contemporaine. The two first volumes, L'Orme du Mail and Le Mannequin d'Osier, were written prior to the Dreyfus Affair. The latter two, L'Anneau d'Améthyste and M. Bergeret à Paris, were written while the case was in progress.

Debré seems to be under the impression that Worms-Clavelin was meant to personify public officialdom at its finest. Unfortunately, we have reason to question that assumption. But before we go into the matter any further, let us at the very outset clear Anatole France of any suspicion of anti-Semitism. His irony, his amibguity, and his mock seriousness are no reflection on Worms-Clavelin's Jewish origin. Anatole France simply wants to portray a high official of the "Opportunist" clique. Fate ordained that he should have encountered a very popular politician of this type who just happened to be Jewish. Worms-Clavelin is patterned on the prefect Hendlé, a friend of the French statesman Léon Gambetta. Close to circles of high finance, he works for the aim of the "Opportunists" which, according to Anatole France, is "to seal off the road to progress." France does not, then, regard Hendlé as the glorious prototype of the Republican who rears a whole new generation of great public officials.[32] Instead, he reduces his protoype to the level of a Homais-type individual.[33] Worms-Clavelin is a rigid, unimaginative personality. France makes frequent snide remarks about the prefect's "metaphysical incapacity" and his utter lack of imagination. Sure of his administrative talents, Worms-Clavelin describes the people of his province as a "splendid group of constituents."[34] Just the same, he is taken for a ride by the Abbé Guitrel, in whom he has placed complete confidence. Under an agreement between the two, the Abbé is promised the prefect's support for his candidacy for an episcopate upon the condition that he, the Abbé, will stop the clairvoyant Deniseau from spreading her anti-Republican prophecies. But once he has become bishop, Guitrel plays a trick on his matter-of-fact friend. Here France underlines the folly of joining forces with the Church and the clergy.[35]

[32]*Le Siècle,* Feb. 9, 1900; *Le Temps,* Feb. 9, 1900.

[33]Character in Flaubert's *Madame Bovary;* personification of the bourgeois fool dabbling in literature and science.

[34]*L'Orme du Mail,* p. 319.

[35]Cf. J. Levaillant, *L'Évolution Intellectuelle d'Anatole France* (The Intellectual Development of Anatole France), p. 466. Guitrel pretends to be favoring the Jews; at the same time he points out that the Jews as a people have been cursed by God. However, he grants that the curse does not apply to Jewish individuals who have accepted Christianity.

Like most of the Jewish female characters in nineteenth-century French literature, the prefect's wife has no typically "Jewish" traits. Raised in humble circumstances, she resembles many other Parisian women who share the bed and board of gentlemen of more privileged origin. In his style, which hides irony behind a mask of good-naturedness, France tells us how the lady had met Worms-Clavelin:

> Madame Vacherie, one of those petty retailers who liked her, acted as a go-between for her and M. Théodore Worms-Clavelin, a young, industrious and promising bachelor of laws who, having found her to be serious and useful in employment, married her after the birth of their daughter Jeanne. In return, she had skillfully maneuvered him into the government.[36]

Mme. Clavelin, efficient as she was, must have been bitterly disappointed when the agreement between her husband and the priest, for whose promotion she had really put herself out, turned sour.

Like many Paris hoydens, Mme Clavelin is keenly intelligent and very charming, and knows how to climb the social ladder quickly and how to maintain her status. She devotes all her talents to helping her husband in his career. But despite the tact and discretion with which she serves her husband's purposes, she cannot help looking at him with a certain amount of condescension. It is a tender, protective attitude. Even when she is unfaithful to him, it is all in a day's work; she does not seem to be enjoying her escapade.

Except for some good matrons and one ardent Zionist, the other female characters cited by Debré do not seem to be obvious "Jewish" types. Courtesans, society women who have converted or are about to convert to Christianity, are not typical of the Jewish community. There is only one trait which they all have in common and which, according to generally accepted opinion, is "Jewish," and that is their beauty. "French gallantry or Aryan susceptibility to female charms," Leroy-Beaulieu said, "has always had a soft spot for their

---

[36] *L'Orme du Mail* pp. 41–42.

long-lashed, velvety eyes. I do not know if anybody is an anti-Semite when it comes to women."[37]

Jean-Paul Sartre, in our own day, does not share that view of the Gentile male's attitude toward Jewish women, whom Chateaubriand was generous enough to absolve of the guilt of deicide. According to Sartre, the phrase "a pretty Jewess" has a definite sexual connotation which smacks of rape and submission or, at best, of self-immolation to escape disgrace.[38]

As for the examples of Jewish cosmopolites cited in De-bré's study, it must be said that his choice was not judicious throughout. Elzéar Bayonne[39] and Crémieux-Dax are not "nice" Jewish characters, as Debré would like to believe. De Vogüé and Bourget both wanted, rather, to present an uneven mixture of Messianism and socialism which is out of character with the French spirit. Crémieux-Dax's best friend Jean drops him because Crémieux-Dax, the Jew, has nothing to offer to a Frenchman who prefers to seek comfort in the bosom of the Church. The hero of Vandérem's *Deux Rives* is a more appealing character; he aspires to genuine Jewishness coupled with active solidarity with all men, regardless of religion or of their attitude toward the Jews. In addition to the cosmopolites, Debré shows us Zionists in Alexandre Dumas' *La Femme de Claude* and Enacryos' *La Juive*.

Daniel in *La Femme de Claude* is a visionary who fore-sees the return of the Jewish people to Palestine at an early date. Leroy-Beaulieu prefers him to Lessing's' Nathan the Wise. "Lessing," he asserts, "is not the only author who dares to show us a Jew upon a pedestal of virtue. To his Nathan the Wise, the virtuous logician, surrounded by a chilly halo of wisdom, I prefer Daniel of *La Femme de Claude,* a Jew who is much more idealistic than the Paris jackanapes would have thought a Jew to be. I have encountered this type myself—but far away from here, in the East [of Europe]."[40] Leroy-Beau-

---

[37]Leroy-Beaulieu, p. 333.
[38]Sartre, *La Question Juive,* pp. 58–59.
[39]Hero of de Vogüé's novel *Les Morts qui Parlent.*
[40]Leroy-Bealieu, *op.cit.,* p. 332.

lieu's enthusiastic reaction to Daniel seems to have been inspired by the perfect harmony of heart and intellect this character personifies. It was certainly not Leroy-Bealieu's intention to convey the idea, which Abraham Dreyfus viewed with such alarm, that a French Jew should be equated with a mere *Ostjude*. Then, of course, there is the ticklish question of the Return to Jerusalem which, in Dreyfus' opinion, should be of no concern whatever to good French Jews. It is this attitude which leads Dreyfus to poke fun at Dumas for having turned Daniel and his daughter Rebecca into veritable angels who become pioneers in the return to the Holy Land.

"Thirteen years ago," Dreyfus says, "when he first produced *La Femme de Claude*,[41] the noted writer wanted to send us off to Palestine. . . . But it appears that, appealing though they were, Daniel and Rebecca did not succeed in winning over most of the Jews who were firmly established in Paris."

Dreyfus is very much surprised that anyone should believe in a literal interpretation of the passage in the Passover Haggadah speaking of the Return to Jerusalem. In his opinion, that pious wish alludes to a strictly spiritual Jerusalem, to the Messianic Jerusalem envisioned by the Prophets for that day when all the nations, having renounced their hatreds, will be united in worship of the same God. The terrestrial site of that Jerusalem could be anywhere on earth—it could even be Paris, if the nations, joined in brotherhood, would agree to accept that city as the capital of the world.

"But while waiting for that day," Dreyfus insists, "the Israelites, who are well off here [in Paris] have no desire to leave this place."[42]

As a matter of fact, what annoys Abraham Dreyfus is not the longing of the *Ostjude* for the land of his fathers, but rather the embarrassment that could come to the French Jews if they were to be lumped with that group of dreamers.

But undesirable though it may have seemed to Western Jews, the Zionist idea found an increasing number of ad-

---

[41] *La Femme de Claude* first appeared in 1873.
[42] A. Dreyfus, *Le Juif au theatre, op. cit.,* pp. lxvi–lxvii.

herents, including some of the best and noblest defenders of the Jewish cause.

It is interesting to read the testimony of Maurice Le Blond, Emile Zola's son-in-law, showing the novelist's interest in the Zionist idea. This is quite in character with Zola's curiosity about ideological novelties and with his intuitive sense for problems of a later age.

Maurice Le Blond recalls the last visit which he, then a young writer, paid to the master, whom he had revered and loved long before he could have nursed expectations of becoming a member of Zola's family. Touching on the problem of *Justice,* the final volume of *Quatre Evangiles,* which was then in preparation, Zola confessed that he was particularly interested in Zionism. "He even told me that he might make a trip to Palestine which, however, he did not contemplate without some qualms. The idea of a chance to inject a sudden new exotic note into his writings intrigued him. He felt a need to refurbish his palette, and such a trip seemed a perfect opportunity to do that. This book, based on scientifically established facts, which would have spoken in general terms about justice in interhuman and international relationships, would have been at the same time, an epic poem and a bold preview of things to come."[43]

Once Zola had familiarized himself with Judaism and had shared its sufferings, he must have felt the existence of a link, imperceptible but real nonetheless, between the fate of the Jewish people and that of mankind. It is not surprising, then, that in his desire to help all of mankind, he should have felt it his task to shed new light on the complex Jewish problem. Whether he realized it or not, the fact is that Zola's eyes were on the mysterious Orient, of which he had retained indelible impressions through his study of the Bible."[44] His vision of justice grew broader and caught up with that of the Prophets. He felt the need to "revisit" the Holy Land, deserted, laid waste, shamed, but still living and quickening, be-

<hr />

[43]Maurice Le Blond, "Les personnages juifs dans l'oeuvre d'Emile Zola," *Revue de Genève,* 1936, IV, p. 314.
[44]The *ébauche* for *Docteur Pascal* shows evidence of this (Ms. N.A.F. No. 10344, Natl. Library, Paris).

cause it was from there that truth would spring forth. Such were the ideas that sprouted in the brain of this defender of justice when his life was so cruelly cut off.

It appears that such ideological trends involving the Jewish problem in the general human context concerned Debré no more than did the intrinsic qualities of the Jew. What interested him was simply the extent to which nineteenth-century French authors subscribed to the total assimilation of the Jews of France. Debré seems to have been annoyed by the fact that even the philo-Semitic writers bestowed typically Jewish names on their Jewish heroes in order to set them apart from Gentile characters. He, for one, saw no valid reason why this particularism should continue; after all, the French Republic, whose climate favored unbelief, had won a striking victory over all religion in general and the Jewish faith in particular. Nobody wanted to pass up the advantages of modern life for the sake of a mass of out-dated rules.

Unfortunately, however, there was no way of ignoring the growth of a development that placed an alarming obstacle in the path to assimilation—racial discrimination. Debré ends his study with a brief mention of this new phenomenon. For the racists, he says, the Jew is different from other men not only by virtue of his name but by virtue of his entire mentality and behavior. Accordingly, the new racism threatens to retard the integration of the Jew into French society.

Hanukkah, 1969   Anna Krakowski

PREFACE

A glance at world literature reveals—in addition to other classic figures—two well-known Jewish characters: Nathan the Wise and Shylock.

Nathan represents an idealized type of Jew. He extends the hand of brotherhood to Christians and Moslems alike across the barriers of religion and education which separate them and which he dismisses as the work of mere mortals. His thinking and conduct are consistently motivated by true piety and love for his fellowmen. In short, he is a blessing wherever he can make his influence felt.

Not so Shylock. He regards his own people as a holy nation, but hates the Christians. He will not eat, drink or worship together with Gentiles. Unable to forgive the man who has insulted him and his people, Shylock is consumed by a thirst for revenge which overrides even his greed and fills him with murderous intent so that good men turn away from him in disgust.

Are we to pity this type of Jew as an unhappy human being who, after having been driven to desperation by insults and injustice, has been cheated of his chance to exact revenge for the wrong he has suffered, or are we to view him as a common usurer who should be unmasked and punished for his evil deeds?[1]

[1]Cf. Carrington: *Die Figur des Juden in der dramatischen Literatur des 18. Jahrhunderts* (The Image of the Jew in 18th-Century Dramatic Literature). Doctoral dissertation. Heidelberg, 1897.

21

John Hales[2] holds that Shakespeare had intended to portray the extent to which the Christians were to blame for the evil traits of men like Shylock. Even gentle, kindly Antonio, Hales points out, has nothing but cold contempt for Shylock, and Shylock's famous speech; "Signor Antonio, many a time and oft in the Rialto you have rated me about my moneys and my usances;" elicits more sympathy for Shylock the Jew than for Shylock the merchant. Shylock's virtues, such as his devotion to his people and his love for his daughter, keep us from condemning him as a completely hopeless villian. True, Shakespeare shows us Shylock at his worst, but at the same time he presents the circumstances that have made him the man he is.

Both Nathan and Shylock cast their giant shadow over the literature of the eighteenth century and that which has followed. From that time on we note that authors have been taking a growing interest in Jewish characters, and the colorful array of figures that people the stage has come to include an ever increasing number of Jews—not only in Germany and England, but also in France.

In his treatise *Le juif de l'histoire et de la légende,* Isidore Loeb[3] comments as follows on Edmond Harancourt's French adaptation of *The Merchant of Venice.*[4]

> I must pay tribute to M. Harancourt, the author of the French drama based on Shakespeare's play. He has treated it as a work of art, and has addressed himself to his task with a high sense of mission, without trying to achieve cheap success through vulgar sensationalism.

In eighteenth-century drama and literature, however, the Jew is still found mostly in comedy. True, he is no longer painted in black colors as a Host desecrator, but he is almost always portrayed as a comic figure, so that any characterization that does not make his Jewish traits too obvious is con-

---

[2]John Hales, "Shakespeare and the Jews," *English Historical Review,* October 1894.

[3]Isidore Loeb, *Le Juif de l'histoire et de la légende* (The Jew in History and Legend), Paris, 1890.

[4]See also Dugué's adaptation, *Le Juif de Venise* (The Jew of Venice).

sidered complimentary.[5] Only after the beginning of the nine-teenth century do we first encounter Jews of many different types in French drama and particularly in the French novel.

The French Revolution gave the Jews new self-confi-dence. Previously their behavior had been that of slaves, but the Revolution had turned them into men.[6] On September 27, 1791, Pierre Samuel Dupont called on the French National Assembly to enact a law giving the Jews of France full citizen-ship rights. The assembly adopted Dupont's motion with thundering applause and, on November 13, 1791, Louis XVI gave his assent to the conferment of full equality on all the Jews in his kingdom.[7] Thus the day dawned when the Jews made their entrance into society and were recognized as full-fledged human beings, who were fed with the same food and were hurt by the same weapons as all the rest of mankind.

It is only natural that this fundamental change in the political and social status of the Jews of France should have been reflected also in French literature. Delivered from the op-pressive atmosphere of the ghetto and free to enter any profes-sion of his choosing and to associate with his Christian fellow-men, the Jew came to play less and less of a comic role in liter-ature, although he was at times still cast in that light. The au-thors of the nineteenth century came to know some Jews who, fired with high idealism, dreamed of world-wide brotherhood, and others again who were zealous patriots, ready to make the supreme sacrifice for their fatherland. The Jewish capitalist and the Jewish banker were still portrayed as crude material-ists who had little use for ideal values and many a time aroused the reader's revulsion, but they were no longer pre-sented as the hagglers and the common cut-throats of bygone centuries—at least not by those authors whose vision re-mained unclouded by partisan disputes. The Jew of nineteenth-century literature was no worse than his Christian rival, and,

as if to compensate for those cases in which the Jew was still

[5]Cf. Dejob, *Le Juif dans la Comédie au XVIII siècle* (The Jew in 18th-Century Comedy), Paris, 1899.

[6]George Brandes, *Die Reaktion in Frankreich* (The Era of Reaction in France), pp. 12 ff.

[7]Heinrich Graetz, *History of the Jews.* Chapter on the French Revolution.

painted in less than bright colors, the playwrights and novelists of the nineteenth century endowed their female Jewish characters with an aura of irresistible charm.

In view of the foregoing, it was felt that a detailed study of the manner in which the Jew was presented in nineteenth-century French drama and fiction should be a subject of interest. To some extent, the attitude of French authors toward the Jews might be taken as an index of the fairness and liberality of Frenchmen in general in this regard, and could shed an interesting new light on the development of French thought on racial and religious differences. At first glance, it might appear that this development could best have been traced by proceeding in a strictly chronological order. But although this method was at first contemplated, it was discarded as the research progressed. For in view of the fact that the actual development does not proceed in an unbroken ascending line, a rigidly chronological arrangement would not have made for a systematic presentation. (More about this at the conclusion of the study.) As a consequence, it was decided, instead, to arrange the material according to subject matter, in two basic categories—anti-Semitic literature and philo-Semitic literature.

PART I.

ANTI-SEMITIC LITERATURE

Chapter 1: The Jewish Money Man

Honoré Balzac (1799-1850) was the first nineteenth-century French author to assign a specific role to the Jews. The unique gift of observation with which that sensitive judge of human character was endowed embraced even this insignificant minority group in the population of France. True, Balzac still saw the Jew primarily as a money man but, unappealing though that character had to be, Balzac, realist that he was, approached him with much human understanding.

Baron Nucingen, in Balzac's novel[8] *La Maison Nucingen*, is a financial genius. Starting out as a mere clerk in the employ of a banker named Aldrigger, Nucingen soon outdistances his good-natured but indifferently endowed employer to become the leading banker in France, while his former employer is faced with utter ruin. Although Nucingen is a law unto himself, he has the reputation of being an honest man. He promptly comes to the aid of his erstwhile benefactor and looks after the Aldrigger family in a most generous way.

Balzac considers the ups and downs of high finance entirely natural. "If stocks rise and fall," he writes, "if values augment and decrease, this flux and reflux is produced by

[8]Balzac, *La Maison Nucingen*, Paris, 1842–47.

some mutual atmospheric movement brought about by the influence of the moon and the great Arago is culpable in not giving any scientific theory for this important phenomenon."

In *Gobsec*[9] Balzac features a Jewish capitalist who has a penchant for philosophizing. Born on the outskirts of Antwerp, the son of a Jewish mother and a Dutch father, Gobsec does not identify with any religion. No one knows whether he is rich or poor; his cash assets are deposited in the vaults of a bank. As he travels all over Paris to cash his bills of exchange, Gobsec gains insights into the hidden recesses of the human heart. He becomes involved in the lives of others, and sees the stark realities of these lives unfold before his eyes. Calmly and placidly he watches his clients totter on the brink of disaster. Unmoved by their desperate pleas, he insists on collecting his debts, even if it means hounding a debtor to death. Gobsec is thoroughly convinced of the irrefutable rightness of the principle which motivates his every act: gold is a commodity which can be sold dearly or cheaply, depending on circumstances, without coming into conflict with one's conscience. In his eyes, a capitalist is one who, by virtue of the high yield he draws from his investments can, and does, take part in any undertaking he considers profitable. But apart from his principles and his philosophical views of human proclivities, once he has put his business concerns aside for the day, Gobsec, at least in the honest opinion of his "advocate"—is the most honorable and tender-hearted of men. "In him, two men are combined in one person; miser and philosopher in one, he is petty and magnanimous at the same time."

The Jewish woman, too, is assumed to possess a certain weakness for the idol Mammon. Accordingly, Alphonse Daudet (1840–1897)[10] put into his novel *Les Rois en Exil* a half-Jewess, who in her contemptible greed will stop at nothing to attain her ends. Sephora is one of the few female Jewish characters in modern French literature to be shown as an obnoxious personality. The novel relates the dreary existence

[9]Balzac, *Gobsec*, Paris, 1842–47.
[10]Alphonse Daudet, *Les Rois en Exil*, Paris, 1879.

of the exiled royal family of Illyria. King Christian, his wife Frederica and their sick, puny child are compelled to flee when republican forces take over their country. Actually, it is Frederica who rules the roost, for Christian is completely under the spell of a passionate youth of twenty. The miserable kinglet is surrounded by strong-willed women who keep "pulling the strings" behind the scenes. The most powerful of these ladies is Sephora Leemans.

Sephora's parents are junk dealers on the Rue Eginhard, an alley in the slums of Paris. Leemans is not a Jew, but a Belgian Catholic, so that Sephora is only a half-Jewess who happens to have the eyes and complexion typical of the Jewish race. A clever girl, she is a good businesswoman by the time she is fifteen. Although her parents take little notice of her, Sephora remains sensible, level-headed and impervious to any temptation to stray from the "straight and narrow." She leaves home early each morning to work as a salesgirl, contributing her meager wages to the support of her parents. Denying herself even the most modest of pleasures, she is content as long as her parents are happy. Then one day, Leemans sells her off to an old baron, much as he would his best showpiece. Three years later, however, Sephora leaves this man, whom she never loved, and conceives a deep affection for an Englishman, a Gentile by the name of Tom Lewis. Lewis sets up an agency, and Sephora is the life of the enterprise. She is willing to make any sacrifice, no matter how great, for her new husband, whom she adores. She is so much taken with Lewis, who "looks more like a monkey than a man," that she remains devoted to him even after ten years of humdrum marriage. King Christian falls into the clutches of this businesswoman. Lewis and his wife attempt to talk Christian into giving up his claim to the throne in return for 200 millions offered him by the Representative Assembly of Laibach. In order to bring Christian to do their bidding, Sephora and her husband lay plans to burden the weak-kneed monarch with a debt heavy enough to push him to the brink of financial ruin. But this, too, requires a spur—in the form of a woman.

Sephora has become as unemotional as her husband. She keeps her sangfroid no matter what befalls, and has some to consider even love purely a matter of business. Completely under the spell of her husband's clever irony, she has made all his ambitions her own, and has eyes and brains left only for money. It turns out that this amazing woman is ruled by the basest of passions. She volunteers to tighten the noose around the ex-king's neck herself. In order to stir the king's passions she pretends to be cold and unyielding. Spellbound, Christian becomes a slave to all the whims and fancies of this demonic woman. Together with him, Sephora squanders more money than her husband and her father can raise and before long she has got Christian to a point where he is ready to give up his royal purple to help pay his debts. Meanwhile, however, Frederica has managed to muster weapons and troops for a campaign against Dalmatia. Even Christian has plucked up enough courage to leave Sephora and join his wife in her venture. But Sephora learns of her pseudo-lover's plans shortly before his scheduled departure. Since she must get back her money and the funds advanced by her husband and her father, she follows Christian and manages to keep him at Fontainebleau one more night. Meanwhile, arrangements are made to trap the king. When his train pulls into the station at Marseilles, Christian II is placed under arrest by a security police inspector. The king escapes trial and punishment by signing an instrument of abdication, relinquishing his throne in favor of his son. This breaks the knot so connivingly tied by Sephora. Christian, overjoyed, rushes to his mistress to tell her that he has abdicated his throne and that he is now free to become hers forever. To his consternation, Sephora treats him with utter contempt and sends him away. She is embittered at all her wasted effort and sacrifice, but she is also cured of a passion which did not stop even at crime.

In the play based on the novel, Sephora's father, the junk dealer, is not a Catholic but a Jew, making Sephora a full Jewess. In contrast to her role in the novel, Sephora in the play is portrayed as Jewesses usually are in the French drama of that period. The father is unappealing, but the daughter is a ravishing beauty and a thoroughly nice person.

René Maizeroy (René Jules Jean Toussaint)* has created a similar character in his novel *Le Capitaine Bric-à-Brac*.[11] Here an army paymaster has become infatuated with a Jewish woman and buys old porcelain and glazed earthenware from her with regimental funds entrusted to him for safekeeping. However, he finds out before long that she is taking advantage of him. He is rescued from utter disgrace and ruin by his mother-in-law, who sells her title to a wealthy merchant in order to save his honor.[12]

In *Les Monachs*[13] Robert de Bonnières shows the Jewish capitalist as a parvenu. Monach has only one appealing character trait: he is good to his mother. The old woman—the most original Jewish character in the novel—has remained true to her ancestral faith and finds solace in her loneliness by reading prayers with a young cantor whom her son has engaged for this purpose. Out of genuine love and respect for his mother, Monach observes many a religious precept for which he himself no longer cares; he keeps the Jewish holidays and at times eats kosher food. He is his mother's favorite, and has shown intelligence and initiative at an early age. After living in Frankfurt am Main and in Vienna, Monach, his mother, his wife and his daughter end up in Paris. There, Monach is fortunate enough to make a number of brilliant business transactions, and becomes very rich. However, he cannot shed the traits and mannerisms typical of the *nouveau riche*. Money has meaning for him only to the extent that it can help him play a prominent role in society. He seeks contacts with important people, whom he invites to sumptuous parties such as only a newly-rich robber baron can arrange. His favorite guests are artists, journalists and self-styled counts and barons, and he is indiscreet enough to boast of his beautiful furniture to these men, who are presumably accustomed to luxury.

*1856–1918

[11]René Maizeroy, *Le Capitaine Bric-à-Brac,* Paris, 1883.

[12]Cf. "Der neueste Roman," *Zeitschrift für neufranzösische Sprache und Literatur,* Vol. X.

[13]Robert de Bonnières, *Les Monachs,* Paris, 1885.

However, Abraham Dreyfus notes:[14]

M. de Bonnières has fastened on one detail which he considers typical. Giving his guests a tour of his mansion, Monach calls their attention to his luxurious furnishings, tells them how much he paid for each piece and invites them to feel the silver and silk brocade of a coverlet. "Isn't that just like a Jew?" the author seems to have said to himself as he noted the incident. But in fact it is not "like a Jew" at all. A real "Jew-type" Jew would have been more likely to walk all over the silver and the silk to create the impression that luxury no longer excites him and that he has the very same coverlets also in his stables.

Monach boasts of the important friends he has left behind in Vienna, among whom he includes people he may have seen no more than once in his life. He is convinced that one must talk as "big" as possible if one is not to remain a nonentity forever. When the Feast of Tabernacles approaches, he is terribly apprehensive lest his *sukka** might seem strange to the Gentiles and draw the attention of his guests to his Jewishness. For this reason, he cuts down as much as possible on his entertaining during the week of *Sukkot*.

He ignores Jewish religious law not out of conviction but solely out of a pathetic eagerness to be one with his precious counts and barons—he delights even in rattling off their names and titles. He is not averse to having Roger, the son of a general who is one of his friends, show an interest in his daughter Lia. While Monach is not by any means burning to marry off his child to the general's son at once, he is not blind to the possible advantages of such a match. He believes that prominent Gentile family connections might help him improve his social position. While he likes France, where he has important interests, he is fully aware that the Jews of the country are perpetually being accused of trying to form a state within a state. Monach feels that if the mob were to turn on

---

[14]*Revue des Études Juives,* 1886. Lecture by A. Dreyfus,"Le Juif au théâtre."

*Booth in which observant Jewish families take their meals during the Feast of Tabernacles.

his coreligionists, it would be good for him to have powerful Gentile kin to protect him from the fury of the populace.

Emile Zola, too, has left us a portrait of a Jewish broker.
The characterization is crass, in keeping with Zola's own
character. However, Zola was fair enough to cast a Gentile
jobber side by side with the Jewish capitalist. As a matter of
fact, the Jewish broker is portrayed as a "Gobsec" type, and
it is the Gentile banker who is dragged into the mire of depravity in typical Zola fashion. Moreover, as a counterfoil to
the Jewish financier, Zola introduces another Jew who is
poverty-stricken and consumptive but noble and idealistic
enough to cherish visions of social revolution even on his
deathbed.

Zola's novel *L'Argent* (Money)[15], which gives us a vivid
description of the stock exchange, features two financiers—
Saccard, a Gentile, and Gundermann, who is a Jew. Saccard,
an extravagant and hot-headed libertine, attempts to wrest control of the money market from Gundermann. A bitter struggle
between the two financiers ensues. Unlike Saccard, Gundermann is level-headed and practices moderation in all things;
he has never pursued idle pleasures. The only woman he has
ever loved is his own wife, to whom he was as faithful forty
years before as he is now, when he has no other choice.
Gundermann leads a galley-slave existence; he is at his desk
by five o'clock each morning, amassing wealth without ever
finding time to acquire or to enjoy the things that wealth can
buy. He has no carnal lusts; he is enslaved only by his sense-
less urge to accumulate a pile of millions for no other purpose
than to leave it to his heirs, in the hope that they would, in
turn, add to their inheritance until it would rule supreme over
all the world.

Saccard is filled with a deadly hatred for Gundermann,
the all-powerful ruler over Paris. He foams at the mouth at
the very mention of this Jew, whom he considers his mortal
enemy. In fact, he hates the entire Jewish people, a race
without a country whom he despises as parasites among the

---

[15]Zola, *L'Argent,* Paris, 1890.

nations, sucking the blood and feeding upon the fat of the peoples in whose midst they live. Gundermann, knowing and calculating businessman that he is, turns down Saccard's request that he buy shares in a contemplated "Universal Bank." He has no intention of serving as a stepping stone for Saccard's ascent on the social ladder; indeed, he goes so far as to predict Saccard's' downfall. "He's too impetuous," Gundermann says of Saccard, "he has too much imagination." However, at a crucial moment Saccard is in a position to fix the stock-market rate. By pandering to the right people he gets word of the peace treaty between Austria and Italy before Gundermann can learn of the development as a result Gundermann, the undisputed ruler of the money market, to whom Cabinet Ministers bow and scrape like lowly clerks to their employer, loses eight million francs. Though somewhat disconcerted by the fact that he should have been outwitted by a hot-headed fool like Saccard, Gundermann takes the loss without a word of complaint. Saccard, on the other hand, emboldened by his victory, is spoiling for a showdown. Gundermann, whose strength lies in his unwearying patience and cool, calculating logic, waits calmly for Saccard's next move. In the end Saccard is exposed and sold out by a woman.

Despite his greed, Gundermann is a charitable man. Notwithstanding his addiction to money, he is essentially generous, even if he is not a noble person. He does not kick his erstwhile rival when he is down—not so much because he, Gundermann, is above petty thoughts of revenge, but because he realizes that it is the better part of wisdom to act to put out the fire at his enemy's house so as to keep the flames from spreading to the rest of the neighborhood, since his own home is located there also. Filled with a sense of tremendous strength and power, he even finds it in his heart to pity the spineless jouster who presses on in pursuit of his aims like a gambler who must have his game or a miser who chases after wealth.

Paul Bourget[16] finds little good to say of Justus Hafner,

---

[16]Paul Bourget, *Cosmopolis,* Paris, 1892.

the Jew who has a subordinate role in his novel *Cosmopolis*. "In a constant alternation of ingratiating bright spots and ghastly shadows," wrote Edouard Drumont*, the notorious anti-Semite, "this novelist presents a true-to-life portrait of the duplicity, the cunning and the spuriousness of all that Jerusalem crowd in Paris."[17]

Hafner, a jobber, is indeed an insufferable character, unfeeling and unprincipled. He accepts that religion which will help him get ahead the fastest. Conniving and unscrupulous in his business dealings, he is incapable of genuine friendship. There is something slimy about the man. He loves his daughter Fanny, but at best it is the sentiment a horse breeder might be expected to have for one of his horses that has won the grand prize.

In his novel *Le Baron Vampire* (The Vampire Baron) Guy de Charnaicé"**[18] singles out the Jewish bankers for attack.[19] After having scraped together a couple of millions through some underhand dealings, Reb Shmoul suddenly turns up as Baron Rakowitz in Paris, where he is received with open arms by the nobility. The baron marries Sophie Fuchs, an actress, and uses her to get even with the Vicomte de Landelle, who once treated him with contempt.

A droll figure is introduced in the person of Showten, the little Jewish collector of china and enamelled ware who, having gained access to the drawing rooms of high society as the much-sought-after appraiser of all sorts of odds and ends, has become a celebrity of sorts. Then there is Mrs. Stein, the wife of a stockbroker of shady reputation, who knows how to insinuate herself into the good graces of the young duchesses with whose families her husband does business. Finally we meet the amorous widow Langmann, a Polish Jewess, and Lisa Adler, a Jewess from Germany who was at one time employed as a children's nurse in Warsaw.

*1844-1917
**1825-1909
[17]Edouard Drumont, "The Jews in Literature," from *La France Juive.*
[18]Guy de Charnaicé, *Le Baron Vampire,* Paris, 1892.
[19]Cf. "Der Moderne Roman," in *Zeitschrift für neufranzösische Sprache und Literatur,* Vol. X.

E. Roustane's *Le Juif de Sofiefka*[20] (The Jew of Sofiefka) takes a similar line, except that the scene of this novel is set in Russia. Here one Jewish family brings ruin to an entire village. It all begins when a Jew, half-dead from starvation, collapses one day at the gate of a manor house. Just as an elderly servant is about to remove the man, the owner of the estate appears on the scene. Pitying the Jew, he takes him into his home. A few years later the Jew has taken over the estate lock, stock, and barrel, having ruined the owner and reduced the peasants of the village to beggary. But the Russian peasants who, besides being fleeced, have had to endure unspeakable humiliation from the Jew and his cohorts, suddenly see the light, Furious, they hurl themselves on the Jews. But instead of venting their fury on the Jews alone and plundering them, the peasants indiscriminately kill and burn everything in sight. In the end we see them, utterly spent, staring at the ruins of their own homes.

[20]E. Roustane, *Le Juif de Sofieka,* Paris, 1894.

Chapter 2:   The Evil Jew

Baron von Horn, in Henri Lavedan's* *Prince d'Aurec,*[21] represents a sinister combination of greed and depravity. Prince d'Aurec, an impoverished nobleman, and his wife are forever in financial straits. His mother, a duchess, has sacrificed a large part of her personal fortune for her son but finally, outraged at his lack of thrift and ambition, has cut him off without a cent. It is at this point that von Horn, a Jewish banker, comes to d'Aurec's rescue, not, mind you, out of altruistic motives, but solely to put the prince and especially the princess in his debt. Horn stands by with ill-concealed glee as the frivolous pair sink deeper and deeper into debt. The unscrupulous millionaire is willing to make any financial sacrifice to compromise the honor of the unfortunate princess. But in the end the old duchess dips into her privy purse just one more time to save the honor of her family, the weak-kneed prince pulls himself together, and Horn is forced to flee in disgrace from his righteous wrath.

In this connection, mention should be made of the farces by Gyp (Sibylle Martel de Janville, Comtesse de Mirabeau), which have been published under the title *Les Gens Chics* (The Smart Set).[22] Since the Jewish characters in these sketches are not portrayed in depth, there is no way of making a detailed study of these individual personalities. Suffice it to say that, in addition to platitudes and ribald jokes, the book contains caricatures of Jews illustrated by cartoons which comprise the major part of the volume. The men are shown gesticulating wildly as they talk, and their noses are long and crooked; as the author puts it, their birth certificates are written all over their noses. Most of the women are on the corpulent side.

[21]Henri Lavedan, *Prince d'Aurec,* Paris, 1885.
*1859–1940
[22]Gyp, *Les Gens Chics,* Paris, 1895.

Zola's novel *Paris*[23] features an antitype to the depraved Baron von Horn. She is a beautiful Jewess whom her father, Justus Stunberger, has married off to the son of a Gentile competitor, Baron Duvillard, in order to escape financial ruin.[24]

Duvillard is a bold, ruthless speculator, generously favored by fortune. Indifferent to his religion, he had no scruples about marrying a Jewess and did not expect her to join the Church. However, several years prior to the point at which the novel begins, his wife converted to Christianity of her own volition in a pompous ceremony at St. Magdalen's Cathedral with all of Paris society in attendance. Indifferent to religion herself, she has taken the step because she is in love with Baron Gérard de Guinsec, a shabby-genteel young nobleman. But the Baroness is not De Guinsec's only love; the young baron has sentiments of compassion and lively admiration for her daughter Camille, an ugly, hunchbacked girl, whom he eventually marries. As artful as she is unattractive, Camile has made it her life's ambition to steal her mother's beau. Aware of the life her mother leads, she keeps tabs on every meeting and every handclasp between the two.

Camille also has a brother, Hyacinthe. A dreamer full of pedantic, half-baked wisdom, he has no interests outside philosophy. He has his head in the clouds, and he considers developments on this imperfect earth much too picayune to be of any concern to him.

"Jews in the strictest sense of the term; that is, Jews who were born Jewish and have remained true to their Judaism, do not occur in this novel," Ludwig Geiger, the historian of culture and literature, comments. "The Jewish prosecutor in the trial of the anarchist has been introduced only so that the author can make a brief observation on his appearance. Similarly, the author does not stop to give a detailed character sketch of the Jewish banker whose daughter and progeny play so important a role in the book. The principal characters of

---

[23]Emile Zola, (Paris), 1898.
[24]Cf. Ludwig Geiger, "Rezension des Romans" (Review of the Novel), in *Allgemeine Zeitung des Judentums*, 1898.

one part of this novel are a beautiful woman—who is of Jewish descent but has converted to Christianity and is featured as a representative of the smart set in Paris society—and her children, who were baptized in the Christian faith at birth. These characters are not haphazard creations; Zola hardly ever uses creatures of pure fancy. Rather, they are intended to illustrate his theories. In Zola's opinion, the age of justice and honest toil can begin only after outworn notions and morbid conditons have been swept away. On the other hand, he points out that children are products of their upbringing; they are a continuation, or a counterpart of the traits and stimuli that motivated the personalities of their parents. The dominant characteristic of the parents in this novel [the Duvillards] is self-indulgence. In the case of the father this trait manifests itself in a hunger for affection. The same trait makes the children blasé. The girl [Camille] becomes an unyielding egotist, while the boy [Hyacinthe] turns into a disembodied soul and an absurd dreamer. The two character types represented by the Gentile speculator and the daughter of a Jewish jobber are intended to portray the brutality and the perverseness that are the fruits of rotten snobbery. This is not anti-Semitism but simply a statement of philosophy of life: a bad seed cannot yield good fruit."

Chapter 3:   The Jews as an Unassimilable Race

In addition to the money motif, anti-Semitic writers in recent years have increasingly fastened on yet another notion to which Robert de Bonnières has already alluded; namely, that the Jew cannot be assimilated and that there are irreconcilable differences between the Semitic element and "Aryan" society.

Since religion has receded into the background in political and social life, it can no longer be represented in literature as a divisive force of consequence. Accordingly, the anti-Semites now mount their attacks not on the religion of the Jew, but on his race, his Jewish blood which no amount of baptismal water can Christianize. Maurice Donnay has pressed this theme in his play *Le Retour de Jérusalem* (The Return from Jerusalem).

Here the Jewish race is represented by Judith, and the Aryan element by her lover, Michel. Unlike her sentimental swain, Judith is never troubled by irresolution or uncertainty. Her strength lies in perfect harmony between her heart and her reason. She believes implicitly in the supremacy and superiority of her race. Her practical mind is the result of her background; her father is a banker. Widely read, she speaks English, German, Italian and even Hebrew. She has mastered several musical instruments, has passed a series of scholastic examinations with flying colors, and holds a number of university degrees. It is on her way to classes at the Sorbonne that she meets her first husband, a young nobleman named Chouzé. Having taken a fancy to him, she writes his examination for him (she passes with honors, while he barely manages to get by). Consenting to marry Chouzé so that she may become a countess, Judith, ardent Zionist though she is, converts to Christianity. However, her conversion is no more than an empty formality; the Countess de Chouzé remains a Jewess at heart, diligently cultivating her Jewish sentiments, and eager to devote her life to the welfare of her race. Before long, she leaves her Christian count with whom she finds she really has nothing in common, and resumes her typically "Jewish" given name.

Michel, the Aryan, falls in love with Judith, the Semitic woman, because he is fascinated by her character. He leaves his wife, who is a loving companion but whose educational background is inferior to his own. To him, Judith's personality represents a perfect combination of feminine sensitivity and masculine intelligence.

Together, the two lovers make a trip to Jerusalem. The rich banker's daughter's purpose in making the journey is to cleanse herself of every taint of Christianity by worshipping at the Wailing Wall in company with Polish-type Jews. In their first transports of love—their relationship, incidentally, is strictly platonic—the Aryan and the Jewish elements get on quite well together. The Semitic soul-snatcher mothers and soothes the virtuous Aryan who frequently suffers from pangs of conscience at having deserted his lawful wife. In an effort to draw him out of his melancholy moods, Judith urges Michel to become a little more ambitious. "Make an effort," she tells him. "Push yourself forward, assert yourself. That ought to give you satisfaction." But after their return to Paris, a discordant tone creeps into their idyllic relationship. Judith invites only Jews to her salon. Fed up with the tactless conduct of these guests, who have practically taken over his home, Michel requests young Voewenberg, the most impertinent member of the group, to spare him his visits in the future. When Judith speaks up for Voewenberg, Michel's long-suppressed rage breaks forth and he blurts out all his objections to the Jews. The Jews, he says, have never been more than peddlers of the ideas of others. They are neither creative nor inventive. They might be strong on intelligence and willpower, but physical prowess has no less a claim to admiration than intellectual gifts. As a matter of fact, the gift of intelligence, in itself, is not worthy of admiration at all unless it goes hand in hand with noble sentiments. And the Jews, in Michel's opinion, may be practical and realistic, but they are also exploiters—tactless, noisy, and utterly without shame.

Michel learns to his dismay that Judith is attempting to "sell" Voewenberg to a Cabinet Minister who has a secretarial appointment to fill. This is the last straw; Michel and Judith both have had enough. Judith particularly, who craves variety in her life, has grown tired of her Aryan swain with whom, as with Chouzé, she now feels she no longer has anything in common. The two ex-lovers part and Judith delights in her newly-won freedom to play hostess to her beloved coreligionists whenever she pleases.

Critics have pointed out[25] that there would have had to be a quarrel betwen the two lovers even if Judith had not been Jewish. We agree; Judith could just as well have belonged to a race other than the Jews.

Voewenberg, Afker and Dr. Lurdau, the swells in Judith's drawing room, are witty, gifted libertines who are out to enjoy themselves before seizing power. All three are anti-militarists and unpatriotic. Dr. Lurdau, in fact, has written an article calling attention to signs of decadence in the French people and seeking to justify his attitude by asserting that, as a true citizen of the world, he has the right to dabble in ethnography and ethnopsychology without regard for anybody's sensibilities.

In *Le Retour de Jérusalem* which, according to the periodical *Gil Blas*,[26] was intended to unleash a *mort aux Juifs* ("Death to the Jews") campaign among the masses, the one character who seems to be portrayed in an appealing light is a Jew named Lazare Hendelsohn.

Hendelsohn, a good Jew, a highly cultured and honest man, faithful friend and Messianic visionary, devotes all his huge fortune to one great cause. He wants to help preserve the purity of his race so that it may survive to fulfill its destiny. However, this noble Jew, who cherishes visions of the brotherhood of all mankind is, in fact, a staunch anti-Semite though, strange as it may seem, he is at the same time an avowed

[25]See preface to *Le Retour de Jérusalem*.
[26]*Gil Blas*, December 8, 1903.

particularist who strongly identifies with his coreligionists. Donnay considers this a serious flaw in the character of the Jews, and says so on practically every page of his play.

In all likelihood Maurice Donnay's Dr. Lurdau, who is a writer, was intended to represent Max Nordau.[27]* As Nordau himself put it,[28] "It seems that Donnay wanted to place me upon the stage as one of the grotesque Jewish characters in Judith's salon. The name [Dr. Lurdau] is suggestive of my own, and the actor who plays the part has assumed my head or, more accurately, my beard. [However], I failed to recognize myself in the play, for the things Donnay puts into the mouth of my supposed double are the very opposite of all that I have ever thought, written or said. If he can find no better way to run me down than by transforming me into my complete opposite, that would be the finest compliment a courtly flatterer could possibly devise. But as regards my beard, I have no copyright on it, and I will therefore gladly leave it to Donnay if he feels he cannot do without it in his play."

The anti-Semitism shown by A. Guinon[29] in his comedy *Décadence* exceeds even that of Donnay. While Donnay's *Retour de Jérusalem* is still being performed, Guinon's play has been banned from the stage in the interest of public peace and tranquillity. While Donnay knew enough to preserve at least the externals of decency and remained a parlor anti-Semite, Guinon vociferously preaches the most vulgar brand of gutter anti-Semitism.

In *Décadence,* as in Donnay, we see the Aryan element revolting against the Asian, except that in Guinon's play positions are reversed: the man is the Asian and the woman is the Aryan. The elder Strohmann is the son of an Austrian shoemaker who is probably of Polish descent. Starting out as a humble trading Jew, he gradually works his way up in the world. After engaging in slave trade in Egypt he settles in Paris, where he sets himself up in the banking business and

---

[27]Max Nordau, author of *Conventional Lies of Our Civilization* (*Zionist leader, 1849−1923).
[28]*Neue Freie Presse,* December 8, 1903.
[29]A. Guinon, *Décadence,* Paris, 1901.

defrauds the people of Paris of their hard-earned savings. His son Nathan is a Jew of the new generation; he typifies the well-established Jew who lives in a stately mansion and has acquired an extensive education at institutions of higher learning. Like Ephraim Monach in De Bonnières' novel, the elder Strohmann, having acquired all the wealth he can use, seeks entry into high society. His sole ambition now is to be admitted to that social stratum to which he refers as the *grand monde*. To this end he acts to arrange a marriage between his son Nathan, and Jeannine, the daughter of a marquis. The nobleman, who is badly pressed for money, readily agrees to the proposal. Nathan courts the girl. He is refused several times but, being somewhat deficient in self-respect (Guinon considers lack of self-respect to be a prominent Jewish trait), he presses his suit over and over again. In order to spare her family the ignominy of financial ruin, the girl finally gives her consent, but her commitment to Nathan Strohmann does not stop her from continuing her flirtation with a lover of Aryan provenance. Nathan's mother, a counterpart of old Mme. Monach, sides with the rabbi against the marriage, but although she seems to rule the roost, she cannot prevent the couple from going through with the wedding. Outraged at the reprehensible conduct of her daughter-in-law—to make matters worse, the girl has also shown gross disregard for the value of money—the old lady eventually succeeds in getting her son to have a serious talk with his wife; in fact, she emboldens him sufficiently to consider challenging Jeannine's lover to duel if only he could be sure that he, Nathan, would win. When curtain lectures prove of no avail, Nathan threatens to divorce his wife. That does the trick, for Jeannine is badly in need of money. She therefore bids a sad farewell to her Aryan lover and, in keeping with her strength of character, she casts her lot with the Asian, saying, *"Mon corps est prêt à vous suivre* (my body is ready to follow you)."

Unlike Donnay, who, as we have already pointed out before, says some things even about his most sinister characters that could be construed as praise, Guinon wallows in the muck of sordid gutter anti-Semitism. Except, perhaps, for the ritual murder myth, the play contains practically all the accusations that have been leveled at Judaism through the ages. Guinon's Jewish characters may not be outright murderers, but they are capable of almost any other crime.

There are some similarities between these plays by Donnay and Guinon and a more recent comedy, *Le Baptême* (The Baptism) by Messrs. Alfred Savoir and Nozière.[30] It should be noted, however, that in the anti-Semitic theme of *Le Baptême* racial factors are eclipsed by religious motivations.

The Blochs, who originally hail from Frankfurt am Main, have grown rich and settle in Paris. They are anxious to have their salons frequented by Catholic society. Thus they have already snared the young Count de Croissy, thanks to whose influence they are honored by a visit from no less a personage than the bishop himself, who is out to get votes for his nomination to the French Academy, and souls for his Church. Hélène, the daughter of the family, is so much impressed with this honor that she decides to convert to Catholicism. Her eldest brother, too, converts, but he does not take the whole matter too seriously. Their mother converts out of vanity; her husband takes the step for business reasons. The baptismal rites for all four are performed on the same day; this seems to be an interesting chapter in the history of the Blochs. Afterwards, Bloch, Senior, pokes fun at himself. Only the old grandmother and little Lucien, whom she has raised and who is completely under her influence, are outspoken in their opposition to the family's conversion.

With the bishop acting as the go-between, the Count de Croissy now asks for Hélène's hand in marraige. But Hélène, fully aware that she is wanted only for her money, goes to Lourdes and decides to become a nun. Her father is furious and refuses to make a donation to his daughter's convent; as far as he is concerned, the Bridgegroom Jesus will have to take Hélène without a dowry. Mme. Bloch, however, disabuses her husband of that notion. The contribution, she tells him, is a business speculation like any other investment. If only he will

[30]Alfred Savoir et Nozière, *Le Baptême,* Parsi, 1907.

put his personal feelings aside and donate one million francs
to Hélène's convent, he may soon become the wealthiest
banker in the Catholic world.

The periodical *Messidor*[31] makes the following observation on the play:

> I believe that the authors of *Le Baptême* were not out to
> prove anything. If this play has some hidden purpose, it
> hides it very well indeed. There is no doubt but that the
> authors observed only one specific case. Features of interest
> are the contrasts between merry interludes and family quarrels,
> the intrigues of the bishop and the rigid attitude of the Jewish
> grandmother, M. Bloch's mockery of the Catechism and his
> tender love for little Lucien. *Le Baptême* does not make one
> inclined to turn Jewish, nor, for that matter, to turn Catholic.

The authors themselves deny that their play was inspired
by anti-Semitic thoughts.[32]

"We did not think we had to create an artificial character," they contend. "We had no intention of employing the
services of a logician to express our own thoughts and feelings. We were anxious not to inject ourselves into the play.
We have merely intended to show, in as light a vein as possible, the troubles of a Jewish family faced with serious problems. We wanted to portray dangerous conflicts and distressing
problems through the medium of comedy. It seemed to us that
here was material for a play in a novel style; it was an ex-
periment in satire and sensitivity. We do not know whether
we have been successful. At the first two performances, at
least, we had our audiences laughing, without the house being
divided into two opposing camps. The applause from the anti-
Semites did not draw protests from the liberals. This should
be sufficient evidence that *Le Baptême* does not have the same
tendency as *Le Retour de Jérusalem* or *Décadence*. We claim
kinship with neither M. Maurice Donnay nor with M. Guinon.
Our master, whom we most humbly revere, is Ibsen."

[31]*Messidor*, November, 1907.
[32]*Messidor*, September, 1907.

PART II.

PHILO-SEMITIC LITERATURE

Chapter 1: The Apologetic Novel

Although the Jew has occasionally been depicted in hateful terms as a greedy capitalist and, particularly in more recent times, as a foreign element in the midst of the French people, the majority of French playwrights and novelists view him with sympathetic understanding and even with a certain amount of admiration. They plead that he be accorded tolerance because he is deserving of it. They glorify the self-sacrificing patriotism shown by the Jew, humble citizen and statesman alike. Of course they point out that the Jew may also pursue unattainable goals as a citizen of the world or as a Jewish nationalist, but these Utopian visions only attest to his burning idealism. These writers portray the Jew as an exalted figure in the bosom of his family and sing the praises of Jewish womanhood.

In the novel *La Juive au Vatican* (The Jewess at the Vatican),[33] Joseph Méry (1798–1865) makes a plea for tolerance toward the Jew. This novel reflects the views of liberal French Catholicism. Its title was obviously chosen for sensational effect, for the Jewess in the book appears on the scene only occasionally as a lovely creature; she has no role in the plot. Nor is the story set in the Vatican.

[33]Joseph Méry, *La Juive au Vatican,* Paris, 1892.

45

The story begins about 1838 in a little house on the Tunisian coast. This house is the home of a Jewish family—father, mother, one son and one daughter who is only thirteen—who fled from Smyrna ten years before with the help of a noble Genoese named Santa Scala. Santa Scala, who sails the Mediterranean, is now visiting the family. Just then, the Jews are attacked by robbers who loot the Jewish community by order of the Bey of Tunis after a disastrous crop failure. After a valiant effort to fend off the marauders, the family escapes by fishing boat. Santa Scala takes them aboard his own boat and brings them to Genoa. The brave, self-sacrificing mother is killed by a bullet. During the journey Santa Scala sets forth his views on the Jews and Judaism to her young son Gideon. He is full of admiration for the inheritors of that great tradition who, though exiled, dispersed and enslaved, have remained true to their ancient faith over forty centuries, steadfastly continuing to observe their cycle of traditional festivals from Passover in the spring to the Feast of Solemn Assembly in the fall.

"Seeing this," he says, "a deep compassion grips my heart and even at the sight of the vices of some of them, bestialized by two thousand years of slavery, I say to myself: No, this injustice that has already gone on so long cannot be beyond remedy. It behooves the priests of Christ to give emancipation to the priests of Melchizedek. This dual priesthood must be sacred to all, for, in the words of the prophet king, it must endure forever."

The setting of the second part of the plot is the city of Rome some time after the election of Pope Pius IX. Santa Scala, now a cardinal and one of the most ardent supporters of the victorious Papal candidate, is shown as an advocate of reforms within the Church. One chapter describes the ghetto of Rome and expresses the indignation any lover of mankind must feel when he sees the conditions in that section of the city, where Roman Jews by the thousands have been confined ever since the beginning of the Christian era.

A tendency similar to that of Méry's book is evident in *Le Juif* (The Jew) by Fortunio (Paulin Niboyet, 1825–

1906).[34] In this rather weak novel a Jewish sea captain sets himself up as the instrument of justice, pursuing and punishing criminals. By and large, Fortunio's aim is to show how ambition and will power have enabled the Jews to accomplish a great deal, despite the obstacles that have been placed in their path and notwithstanding the fact that they are still the most oppressed and despised among men.

The 1890's when the Dreyfus case set off a new wave of anti-Semitism, proved a veritable golden age for apologetic novels of this type. This great political struggle, in which the Jews were actually no more than pawns, was not only fought out in political dailies and periodicals but is also reflected in the literature of the time. Thus the Dreyfus case is at the center of Anatole France's *L'Anneau d'Améthyste* (The Amethyst Ring).[35]

Here we find discussions about the Jews in general. A place of particular prominence is given to Mme Bonmont, a converted Jewess, and her son Ernest. Abbé Guitrel condemns the unpardonable error the Jews have committed in not accepting the divinity of Jesus. On this point, he asserts, they have been utterly unyielding. While he allows that the beliefs of the Jews do not run counter to reason, the abbé feels that they should enrich their religion by incorporating the truths of Christianity into their creed. In Guitrel's opinion, the Jewish nation is doomed to perdition, but the Jews as individuals are not, particularly not those individual Jews who convert to Christianity. To hate converted Jews would be at variance with the teachings of Christian charity. In fact, the abbé says he respects even some unconverted Jews for their kindliness and for their generous support of charitable and godly causes. The Christians, he says, would do well to follow the example set by the R. and F. families.[36] He particularly admires Mme Clavelin, for her "heavenly inspirations" even though she has not embraced the Catholic faith. It is to her that the congregational schools of the de-

[34]Fortunio, *Le Juif,* Paris, 1879.
[35]Anatole France, *L'Anneau d'Améthyste,* Paris 1899.
[36]Anatole France uses these initials only.

partment owe their existence. Mme Bonmont, who is on visiting terms with the prefect, has willed most of her wealth to the Church. She is in love with Raoul, an anti-Dreyfusard, who keeps making anti-Semitic remarks in her presence, much to her annoyance because they remind her of her Jewish origin.

Raoul's two friends M. de Brécé and M. Leterrier hate the entire Jewish race, including Jews who have converted. In fact, they dislike renegade Jews even more than they do those who persist in their ancestral faith. In their opinion the French Revolution and the institutions, laws and customs which followed in its wake are to blame for France's Jewish problem, and France can be saved only by a prompt return to the Old Régime.

Bergeret, the quiet scholar and glowing idealist, is the only one in the group to side openly with Dreyfus and with the Jews. He remains firm in his convictions even after almost all of the press has blindly joined in the cry, "Crucify him" as required by the political hue of the papers concerned. Bergeret has nothing but contempt for the misguided mob shouting outside his window: "Down with Zola! Death to the Jews! Down with Bergeret!" He turns away in disgust from the brutish mob which has lynched Meyer, a Jewish trades-man, just to demonstrate its profound respect for the army. Bergeret respects the Jews for their intelligence, but particularly for their adaptability—a trait which many wrongly say they do not possess. There is no such thing as incompatibility between the races, and Bergeret considers racial discrimination a great evil. Race does not make a country, for there is no people in Europe that is not made up of a host of different races. He cites Renan's wise saying: "What welds men into a people is the memory of the great things they have accomplished in the past and the will to accomplish more great things in the future."

Anatole France takes up the cause of the Jews also in his novelette *Le Procurateur de Judée* (The Procurator of Judea).[37] This story is written in the form of a dialogue in which Pontius Pilate, who hates the Jews, and Lamia, who

[37]Anatole France, *Le Procurateur de Judée*, Paris, 1902.

sympathizes with them, exchange views on the subject of Jews and Judaism. Pontius Pilate considers the Jews arrogant and at the same time contemptible. A combination of miserable cowardice and unyielding stubbornness, they are impervious to love and hatred alike. In his opinion, they are insensitive to punishment; the more obstinate among them willingly bend their necks to the executioner's blows. The Jews hate everything Roman, for they regard the Romans as unclean creatures whose very existence is an insult to the Jewish faith. Unlike all the other nations, who have willingly submitted to Rome, the Jews persist in their defiance. They refuse to do military service and withhold their tribute payments so that the authorities are quite literally forced to wrest the money from them.

Lamia suspects that his friend is out to abrogate the laws of the Jews and to compel them to make changes in their traditional customs. "It has pleased you," he tells him, "to strengthen their suspicions and to make no secret of your contempt for their faith and their rituals. But one must admit that even if the Jews have not reached the level of the Romans in the contemplation of things divine, they do observe time-honored mysteries."

Pontius Pilate denies his friend's accusation that he is harboring a futile grudge against the Jewish people which, by defying him, has thwarted Rome and broken the peace. However, he can see where this people will lead Rome. "Since Rome cannot rule over this people," he asserts, "she must destroy it."

There is no doubt, Pontius Pilate continues, that one day these unruly Jews, who are forever plotting rebellion, will unleash a revolt against Rome compared to which the threats of the Parthians will be child's play. The Jews secretly nurture absurd hopes and dream of the ultimate downfall of the Roman Empire, and they will continue to do so as long as they believe in the advent of a prince of their lineage who will come and rule over all the world. "This people is unmanageable," he concludes. "Therefore, it must cease to exist."

Lamia, who has lived in Jerusalem as a curious observer and has freely mingled with the Jews, has noted virtues in them which are unknown to Pontius. He has met meek Jews, whose simple ways and guileless hearts remind him of the songs of the Roman poets, and has seen men die under the whips of the Roman legionnaires without revealing their names, content to lay down their lives for a cause they deemed just. "Such men," Lamia says, "do not deserve that we should despise them. I respect them because one must be fair and moderate in all things."

Edmond Gautier Téramond's novel *La Maîtresse Juive* (The Jewish Mistress)[38] was inspired by the Dreyfus case, as, most likely, were the few observations about the Jews in E. M. de Vogüé's *Le Maître de la Mer* (The Master of the Sea).

La Maîtresse Juive has little to offer in the way of ideas and is crammed with filth. It tells of the fight between a young man named Blaise Delavanche and his mother over Blaise's love affair with Emma, who is Jewish. Blaise is shocked by the anti-Semitism of his family which indiscriminately despises an entire race. He can understand such sentiments in his uncle, an abbé, who may be expected to hate the Jews for religious reasons as the crucifiers of his God. In Blaise's eyes the priest's anti-Semitism is a matter of business in which reason has no part. Blaise is also not surprised that another uncle, a captain in the army, should hate the Jews, for his anti-Semitism simply reflects the military spirit that prevailed in the French army throughout the years of the Dreyfus affair. But he cannot understand why his father and mother should have joined in this racial bickering which was setting human progress back by several centuries. His parents could not have been influenced by an anti-Semitic education or tradition; both of them had Jewish friends when they were young and he, Blaise, never heard that his grandparents had been disturbed about these attachments. Accordingly, Blaise concludes that the constant concern about religion, which has suddenly become the decisive factor in all the social relationships and sympathies of the Delavanches, stems from a new craze rather

[38]Edmond Gautier Téramond, *La Maîtresse Juive,* Paris, 1903.

than from genuine conviction; it seems to be based more on a fad than on real caste or class prejudice. In his opinion, there is no excuse for this sort of anti-Semitism. Therefore, when his mother taunts him, "Go back to your Jewess," Blaise finds himself loving Emma more than ever, not because she is Jewish but because, being Jewish, she personifies to him his own struggle against the narrow, reactionary views of his family.

As we have already noted, E. M. de Vogüé's *Le Maître de la Mer*[39] mentions the Jews only in passing. Here, the question posed is how to keep the Jews from attaining world power. One of the participants in the discussion proposes the enactment of more stringent naturalization laws, and particularly severe anti-Jewish legislation. Tournoël disparagingly likens these measures to sand hills which children pile up at the seashore; in his opinion, they are powerless to stem the tide of events. Some of them are naive, others are ruthless, but they are all ineffective. The only way to deal with the problem, he asserts, is to establish colonies where, like all the aliens who have swamped France, the Jews could be sent to earn wealth by dint of their own effort. The hero of the novel is a clever businessman named Robinson. A man of broad views, he demands for the Jews not mere tolerance, which could be considered as a special privilege rather than as a right, but absolute and unlimited freedom.

[39]E. M. de Vogüé, *Le Maître de la Mer,* Paris, 1903.

Chapter 2: The Jew as a Citizen of His Country

In addition to this apologetic type of novel we encounter literature in which the author is not content merely to defend his Jewish protagonist against some specific accusation, but has him personify a definite ideal or virtue.

Thus Emile Erckmann (1822–1899) and Alexandre Chatrian (1826–1890), joint authors of the novel *L'Ami Fritz*,[40] have viewed the Jews of the Alastian town of Pfalzburg with warm sympathy and affection and have portrayed them accordingly. The Jewish characters in their writings are simple, naive and a little odd, but they are eminently ethical and respectable.

Reb David in *L'Ami Fritz* may be cast in a somewhat petty role, but he is given a chance to show his nobility of character. He has been trying to marry off his Gentile friend Kobus, a confirmed bachelor, and thinks he has finally found the right girl for him. She is Suzel, a tenant farmer's daughter. With the help of his native intelligence, Reb David guides the romance to a happy end. He even has a dowry all ready for Suzel—a fine vineyard which, in fact, he has obtained from none other than Kobus, in payment for a bet the bachelor made with him that he, Kobus, would never get married. Reb David firmly believes that a man can be happy only if he has a happy home life. All other pleasures pale before the joys of domestic bliss. "No—your bachelor joys, your vintage wines, your jokes—they're all meaningless," he says." They are misery compared to true domestic bliss. You can only be truly happy if you have a family of your own, for there you are loved."

In the novel, Reb David has no more than a subordinate part. But in the comedy that is based on the book, he appears as a main character along with Kobus. In the play, Reb David is portrayed in a much more prominent and handsome role. In the novel, David is a good-natured individual with a none-

---

[40]Erckmann-Chatrian (joint authors), *L'Ami Fritz,* Paris, 1864.

too-broad horizon. He has some native intelligence, but it fails him when he is faced with problems more complicated than matchmaking. By contrast, David in the play is an important personality and an idealized type—a good Jew, a fine man and a loyal, patriotic citizen. Both Erckmann and Chatrian were chauvinists; perhaps their play was inspired by their ardent patriotism. Still smarting from the blow of France's defeat in the 1870's, they feared that their country was heading for more humiliation. They viewed the steady decline of France's population as a symptom of her decay. This is the tendency of the comedy, as advocated by David, the Jew, who is a rabbi in Pfalzburg until 1870, when he becomes chief rabbi of France.[41]

Reb David pushes Kobus into marriage not out of a mere predilection for matchmaking, but because he honestly believes that France's survival depends on the virtues of clean, wholesome home life. Reb David never tires of reminding his friends to remember where their duty lies. Every citizen is obligated to raise children who will grow up to be brave men, ready and able to defend their country in the hour of danger. He who derives advantage from his country but is not willing to sacrifice his life and fortune upon its altar is a bad citizen. "Peoples that stop growing in numbers are riding for a fall," Reb David says, "Those which increase and multiply will never go under. The unfortunate Jewish race, hounded and harassed though it is, still survives and is a force with which the rulers of the world must reckon, because it continues to multiply. England and American rule over one half of the globe. The future belongs to those races which multiply, while those which prize empty amusements above the joys of family life will eventually go to ruin and become extinct in slavery."

The play *L'Ami Fritz* first appeared on the stage in 1876 at the Théâtre Français. When the play was first advertised, St. Génest[42] recalled that the authors, to whom Molière's own stage was now being made available for their production, had

[41]*Revue*, 1886. Lecture delivered at the Société des Études Juives.
[42]Cf. *Archives Israélites*, December, 1876.

heaped insults on the French troops that had fought so bravely near Metz during the Franco-Prussian war. Nevertheless,
the première was a huge success, with Paris society present in
full force and applauding thunderously.[43]

The Jew who is an ordinary citizen and whose horizon
in most instances does not extend beyond the limits of his native village can express his patriotic sentiments only in petty,
trifling matters. But when given an opportunity to assume
high public office, the Jew demonstrates his loyalty on a grand
scale, filling responsible positions with diplomatic skill in the
service of his country.

In *L'Orme du Mail* (The Elm on the Mall)[44] Anatole
France features a Jewish statesman, the prefect Worms-Clavelin, who has been appointed to his office at the time of the
Elysée scandals during the presidency of Jules Grévy (1879–
1887). He has lived through the corruption which rears its
head again and again to the detriment of the French parliament and public authority. All that Worms-Clavelin asks of his
constituents is that they remain loyal to the republican régime.
He does not expect them to show zeal or enthusiasm, sentiments which he considers outdated. His own relationship with
the Electoral Committee, the only authority in his department,
is one of strict obedience; he carries out its orders with out-
ward eagerness and concealed defiance.

The Jewish prefect is clever, tactful and popular. An opportunist at first, he develops into a true liberal and staunch
progressive. He favors freedom of speech, but is much too
clever to permit any abuses of that right. As an honest public
servant, he sees to it that no harm should come to the government, and the political situation in his department is excellent.

Clavelin is a friend of Abbé Guitrel, an educated and
urbane cleric. The Jewish official assiduously cultivates this
friendship; he feels flattered at the thought that he, the Jew, is
in a position to patronize one of the priests who have been
trying for eighteen centuries to exterminate the Jews. The

---

[43]Cf. *Archives Israélites*, December, 1876. We do not need to analyze *Le
Juif Polonais* here, since it features only one Jew, who plays no role in the
plot except that he is killed.

[44]Anatole France, *L'Orme du Mail*, Paris, 1897.

man in the shabby soutane is a frequent guest at stately mansions which are closed to Clavelin, the Jew, and the ladies of the aristocracy respect the cassock which grovels before Clavelin's robes of office. The priest, politician that he is, treats Clavelin with deference. In return, the prefect shows him special favor; he loves the priest for his tolerance, liberalism and open-mindedness.

Worms-Clavelin, himself, looks at religion only from an administrator's point of view. He is not a religious man. His parents, likewise indifferent to religion, did not give him any religious education. "He remained empty, colorless and free." Unresponsive to metaphysical concepts, he regards himself as a positivist. An enthusiastic disciple of his field of learning, he bases his views on proven fact alone. Holding forth to the priest on the subject of religion, he pits his own Masonic views against Guitrel's dogma; he rejects the idea that any intelligent person could possibly accept so much as one word of the Catechism. In his official capacity, however, Clavelin tolerates every form of worship.

Guitrel is distressed at his Jewish patron's ignorance and superficiality. Clavelin, for his part, deplores the fanaticism and obstinacy of the clergy of whom he, Clavelin, has been so considerate throughout his term of office, but who complain about being oppressed whenever they are prevented from oppressing others. When the diocese of Tourcoing becomes vacant, Clavelin, as prefect, has considerable say in the naming of a new bishop. He spares no effort to obstruct the nomination of Bishop Lantaigne, whose political views and religious orthodoxy are anathema to him, and gives his full support to the candidacy of Guitrel, the man of moderation and compromise.

Chapter 3: The Jew as a Citizen of the World

Standing as a strange parallel and contrast at the same time to the Jews in the writings of Erckmann-Chatrian and Anatole France is Schleifmann, the Jew in Fernand Vandérem's novel *Les Deux Rives* (The Two Banks [of the Seine]).[45] Like Reb David and Clavelin, Schleifmann, too, is an idealized type. But unlike the patriotic rabbi and prefect who strive for the welfare of France, Schleifmann, the perpetual student, is a fanatical cosmopolite who seeks the welfare of the whole world.

Schleifmann has a touch of anti-Semitism, but it is motivated by his love for his race. He is an anti-Semite in the spirit of the prophets Jeremiah, Isaiah and Amos, condemning those members of his race who try to evade the destiny of their people and pursue shallow pleasures instead of attempting to exert a beneficial influence on the world through the ideas and ideals of Judaism. Schleifmann's Semitic pride makes life difficult for him.

Actually, Schleifmann tends to neglect the observances ordained by the ancient Law of Moses. However, in times of trouble he recalls the faith of his fathers. Thus he recites the traditional Jewish prayers for the dead at the bier of his friend Cyprien. Having embraced socialism, which he regards as the religion of modern times, he considers Karl Marx and Lasalle messengers from God, sent to disseminate this modern gospel on earth. To Schleifmann, the writings of Marx and Lasalle are the modern Bible. He attempts to propagate his ideas and, before long, he is charged with being a pernicious influence on the State. His punishment—three years' confinement in a fortress followed by ten years' exile—puts a damper on his zeal, but leaves him unshaken in his beliefs. Having observed at first hand the growth of anti-

[45]Fernand Vandérem, *Les Deux Rives,* Paris, 1898.

56

Semitism in Eastern Europe, he is convinced that anti-Jewish discrimination will spread to the West also. He has his own ideas, derived from Judaism pure and simple, about the best way of fighting this evil. He says that the wealthy Jews must return to the traditions of their people, whom Providence has given the task to serve as moral, intellectual and religious guides to all the nations. The Jews, he holds, should forsake modern society which has weakened their moral fiber, return to the democratic tradition from which they have sprung, and utilize their exceptional talents for the defense of the under-dog and for the advancement of justice. However, the trouble-some prophet reaps only ridicule from his coreligionists whom even his warnings of the threat of anti-Semitism fail to impress. Anti-Semitism, they insist, could never take root in the land of freedom and revolutions. When his warnings prove all too well-founded, and Gentile envy and resentment breed the poison weed of anti-Semitism even in his country, Schleifmann defends his fellow-Jews against attacks, but can-not help feeling a certain pride at having predicted this out-burst of Jew-hatred all along.

Schleifmann's best friend, Cyprien, is an anti-Semite: it is not unusual for anti-Semites to have Jewish friends. Cy-prien succumbs to the temptation to try his luck on the stock market which, in theory, he detests. When Cyprien loses everything he has, Schleifmann not only places his personal funds at his disposal, but also solicits help from Jewish finan-ciers. When these bankers prove indifferent to Cyprien's plight because he has never taken their advice, Schleifmann takes the opportunity to appeal to their conscience. The Lord, he tells them, has not given them their intelligence that they should waste it on the stock market. He predicts their downfall and warns them that they will drag many innocent people down with them. In reply to their protestations of French patriotism, he tells them that they really have no na-tional loyalties, and that they are indifferent even to their Judaism. They acknowledge their religion only under duress, they bear it without pride and find it inconvenient, particular-ly in club and salon life. Schleifmann agrees that the Christians are just as ruthless in their financial operations as the Jews whom they persecute and revile for the very same tactics. However, he points out, "the Jews are the people of the Lord and must therefore set a good example; they must make do with fewer joys than the other nations, and bear more pain. This is their destiny, a glory which is indeed difficult to attain. But they cannot escape their destiny except at the price of even greater pain."

Elzéar Bayonne, in the novel of Eugène Marie Melchoir de Vogüé,* *Les Morts qui Parlent* (The Talking Dead), is the same distinctive cosmopolitan type as Vandérem's Schleifmann.

Elzéar Bayonne, a descendant of Spanish Marranos, has early outstripped his classmates in school. His first teacher is his grandmother, Sephora, who has taught him to read Hebrew and explains to him the meaning of the customs and observances of Judaism. The child's imagination is stirred by the Bible, the book "which relates the wonderful romance of his race." He becomes acquainted with a host of strong and mighty men who had gone forth from humble beginnings to become the masters of the world—Joseph the slave, Moses the shepherd, pious Daniel, and the beggar Mordecai. Elzéar's uncle, a member of the Institut de France,** gets him a scholarship to the *lycée* where he does as well as he did in public school and where he finds entirely new vistas opening up before him.

The death of his grandmother breaks the last link in the chain that has bound him to the dreams and the miseries of his past. The brilliant rhetorician whose mind is receptive to any new idea, who enthuses over fashionable literature and who is out to conquer Paris, has nothing in common with the little ragamuffin from the Bayonne homestead. Having readily absorbed the unbelief around him, the brilliant student has only ridicule for anyone who presumes to remind him of the precepts of the Torah. In his opinion, that "old rubbish" rates the same indulgent smile as the long-forgotten Catechism of

*1848–1910
**Includes five "Academies."

his non-Jewish classmates. If on occasion he takes a look into the Old Testament, he does so only to satisfy his intellectual curiosity. He meditates on the unusual story of Saul and David, whom he has taken as his models, while his classmates turn to Napoleon as their idol. After his graduation, Bayonne is put to work in a business concern. However, he is disgusted with his position, which he considers petty in view of his ambitions for the future. He is even revolted at the occupation of his father, about which his classmates kept teasing him in high school. As he puts it to his mother, Elzéar feels drawn to the learned professions. Rachel, practical woman that she is, looks straight into her son's eyes, and asks him whether he is sure that this is what he really wants. To this, Elzéar replies that he is sure the others do not know what *they* really want.

Bayonne goes on to study law, political economy and history and before long has made a name for himself as a brilliant orator. However, the years go by without Bayonne's justifying his friends' high hopes for his future. Apparently the fiery ambition which spurred him at the time of his graduation has been dissipated by the playboy life into which he has thrown himself with unnatural abandon. Thanks to his innate talents he becomes popular and gains access to exclusive salons. There, he holds forth on his democratic ideas and the other guests listen indulgently to his inflammatory tirades because he dresses well and cuts a nice figure. Bayonne has come into student circles touched by the winds of Socialism. At first, he falls in with these then-fashionable doctrines out of a sheer desire to follow the crowd, but later he embraces them wholeheartedly of his own accord, and perhaps also for reasons of expediency.

Bayonne discusses his views with his schoolmate Jacques Anderran, an irresolute dreamer. With the ruthlessness of an orator to the manner born, Elzéar overwhelms him with his rhetorical skills. Jacques accuses him of being a traitor to his race which, after all, clearly stands on the side of wealth, the source of its strength. But as far as Bayonne is concerned, there are no races; there are only individuals. "Race," he as-

serts, "is an outdated textbook term." But even if he were to
look at the issue from his friend's point of view, Bayonne
says he would consider it dismal to think of the Jews as a
race whose ideal was the gratification of material cravings.
"Which fighter for humanity," Bayonne demands, "could
ever equal the idealism and the forcefulness of the prophets
of old? With the Jewish people, mankind's age-old lament over
persecution and oppression has been passed on from father to
son, from generation to generation. The righteous wrath of an
Amos has only reinforced my distaste for stupid society."

Bayonne sees Socialism as the one stepping-stone that
still holds promise for the future. He is convinced that all the
other political parties have outlived their usefulness. He believes it should be an easy thing for any Socialist clever enough
to convey an impression of elegance coupled with boldness to
make "Lady Paris" sit up and take notice, and in the end to
conquer her. His brilliant work in a court case brings him into the public eye. Encouraged by his success and riding on the
crest of a wave of popularity, Bayonne starts holding public
meetings. At first his audiences distrust his exaggerated elegance, but the handsome, well-dressed man appeals to the women who soon dispel the misgivings of their menfolk. Elzéar
is elected to represent the city of Paris in the House of Depu-
ties where, thanks to his oratorical skill, he becomes the leader
of the Socialist groups. Most of his listeners applaud his
speeches, which hold them spellbound but do not win them
over to Bayonne's views. However, Bayonne's meteoric career
has the effect with which we are familiar. Now that he is
famous, he forgets about his origins, his family and his race.
If asked who he is, he replies, "I am a Parisian like any other
Parisian, just a little more vigilant."

Bayonne falls in love with Daria, a Christian woman who
shares his views to the point of fanaticism. But at this point
he meets a Jewish actress named Esther, a meeting which sets
off the great conflict of his life.

Rosé Esther[46] who is, in fact, Bayonne's cousin, was considered a child prodigy in her home town. She has run away

[46]E. de Vogüé, Les Morts qui Parlent, Part 2.

from high school, not because she is out for adventure, but because she has given mature thought to her future; she has compared the dreary life of a public-school teacher with the glamor of the theater and its promise of independence, fame and fortune, and has made her choice accordingly. She feels she is no less entitled to make the break than are the male students who quit high school to plunge into journalism. Rose Esther, too, has plans and ambitions. She has not chosen a career on the stage in expectation of riches, or an easy life. She expects much more than that; she aspires to "the true throne of queens." She is persuaded that the only aim held in common by all Parisians is pleasure which, in turn, is offered by only one respectable institution, namely, the theatre. The actress, she asserts, has already become the rival of the most envied and respected ladies of society. The gifted, beautiful actress will be the only feminine influence that will be able to restore order to the tottering world. To the credit of our era, Esther adds one small qualification; namely, that a courtesan could not fill such a role in France's social régime. Without character, respectability, intelligence and culture neither men nor women can produce achievements of consequence. Only the lady of the stage who is armed with these weapons stands a chance of toppling the ancient citadel of France.

For years Esther has played small parts in the theater and it looks as if whatever talent she has is doomed to go undiscovered. She leads a strikingly sedate life, receiving only a small circle of friends who admire her high intelligence, her self-restraint and her benign wisdom. She does not associate with the smart set. Then, one day, playing the leading role in *The Hussites,* she reveals a degree of talent of which no one would have imagined her capable. She is hailed as a great tragedienne and as the hope of French art. Pursued by scholars, actors, playwrights and journalists, Esther accepts her new fame as she would receive a long-overdue visitor whose arrival does not carry any element of surprise. Of the man who come to pay their respects to her on the night of the première, Elzéar Bayonne is singled out for her special attention: she invites him to her home.

During that visit Esther and Bayonne discover that they are related. Esther captivates her cousin with her conversation, which she guides with skill and tact, and in which every word is carefully weighed.

Esther needs this man to fulfill her personal ambitions, but he is of little use to her as long as he remains a mere member of Parliament. To serve her purposes, he must become a member of the Cabinet; but that would bring Bayonne into conflict with his party. Esther therefore sets about to cure him of his Utopian dreams, but to no avail. He counters her arguments with the words of her nihilist rival Daria: "I want to have all men dream my dreams." In order to get rid of Daria, Esther decides to inform her of Bayonne's Jewish origin and goes so far as to tell her that her lover is entertaining notions of becoming a Cabinet Minister. In a talk with Daria, Bayonne proudly admits his membership in a race which he praises as fine and noble. For love of Daria, he gives up his ambition to rise even higher on the ladder of politics. However, he is killed in a duel with a rival who then puts himself at Daria's service.

A philosophy of life identical with that of de Vogüé's Elzéar Bayonne is held by Crémieux-Dax in Paul Bourget's* novel *L'Etape*.[47] Bourget is fair enough to depict Crémieux-Dax, the Jewish democrat, as a man of fine human qualities.

Like Bayonne, Crémieux-Dax comes of a family living in the south of France and tracing its ancestory to the Maranos, who were driven from Spain by King Ferdinand the Catholic at the end of the fifteenth century. He has inherited from his ancestors in the Iberian Peninsula the "deep-set black eyes" which still reflect the blaze of the Middle Eastern sun. He is also liberally endowed with the principle traits that have made the Jewish race unconquerable: a nimble mind, exceptional adaptability, incredible energy, fervent zeal coupled with untiring perseverance, and a strange fierceness tempered by self-interest. A brilliant student, Crémieux-Dax has early adopted Darmsteter's doctrine concerning the identity of the

---

*1852–1935. Bourget was a Catholic and a conservative.
[47]Paul Bourget, *L'Étape*, Paris, 1902.

two concepts which run like a red thread through the history of the Jewish people and through that of human society and revolution. Young Crémieux-Dax believes that Judaism is based on two principal dogmas—the unity of God and the Messianic hope; that is, the oneness of the law and the world, and the ultimate triumph of justice in mankind. These two dogmas promote the advancement of humanity in the present day. Translated into modern terms, they are unity of strength and faith in human progress. But deeply though this revolutionary credo is rooted in his soul, Crémieux-Dax does not act upon it until France is faced with a crisis. From that time on the democratic views of the matured scholar are nourished by powerful motivations. Current developments have clearly shown him the growing alienation of the French people from the principles of the Revolution. Making a cult of its errors, the French people has adopted a policy apparently identical with that of all those who instinctively advocate the formula, *"Fiat justitia, pereat mundus."*

Crémieux-Dax leaves no stone unturned to channel the strength of his people into the service of those ideas which were banned by the bourgeoisie a hundred years before. Whenever someone points out to him that in times of revolution the peaceful citizen takes on a shocking resemblance to the savage, or when someone reminds him of the days of the Commune, Crémieux-Dax, the graduate of the *Ecole Normale,* replies: *"O passi graviora."* At such times "an ironical smile plays about his lips, betraying the afterthroes of oppression and the intellectual courage of a race for which, despite its sufferings, upheavals hold no terror since they are far less cruel than its own age-old misery."

Crémieux-Dax founds the Tolstoy Union, in which he gathers like-minded individuals about him. A noble friendship unites him with Jean, a fellow-Unionist. The two men have been friends since their schools days, with Crémieux-Dax taking the dominant role. With his stable, logical character, Crémieux-Dax exerts a powerful influence on Jean, who is insecure and unstable. It is due to Crémieux-Dax's almost absolute power over him that Jean, sentimental and pious though he is, has joined the Tolstoy Union and becomes embroiled in an inner conflict which keeps him from marrying Brigitte, a girl whom he worships but who is a devout Catholic.

Though he is the heir to a huge fortune, Crémieux-Dax lives frugally, taking simple lunches and suppers with his friends each day. He is impervious to insults from his fellow-Unionists and is ready at all times to make peace in order not to lose an able helper in the cause of his ideals. He is firm only in his efforts to protect sensitive Jean from the barbs of their comrades who can be quite rude at times. For himself, Crémieux-Dax does not care whether he is liked or not, except in the case of a very few individuals, of whom Jean is one.

Crémieux-Dax goes so far as to seek to win Abbé Chanut for the Socialist cause, for he believes that the Catholic Church, as the only organized power in the West, should assume the heritage of the ancient Jewish prophets.

Crémieux-Dax thinks that his Union is unconquerable. At the crucial moment when the organization collapses, he takes the part of "the captain who bravely remains on deck and continues to act calmly and with mature deliberation." When his friend Jean takes refuge in the bosom of the Catholic Church in search of solace for his mental sufferings, Crémieux-Dax sadly bids him farewell. As they clasp hands, never to meet again, Crémieux-Dax says to Jean, *"Idem velle et idem nolle ea demum amicitia est."*

Chapter 4: The Jew as a Zionist

In addition to Jews who advocate extreme ideas of internationalism, nineteenth-century French literature presents the nationalist Jew who gives voice to his longing for Zion.

Thus, as early an author as Alexandre Dumas, fils (1824–95)[48] has a modern-type Zionist in his drama *La Femme de Claude* (The Wife of Claude). Dumas' Zionist is Daniel, a dreamer, but definitely not a chauvinist. Capable of genuine and deep friendship, he shows brotherly love for Claude, a Gentile whose patriotic feelings for France are as strong as Daniel's sentiments for Zion. "It is a good thing to be honest and to esteem each other as we do," Daniel says to Claude as they bid each other farewell. Notwithstanding his penchant for mysticism, Daniel has plenty of common sense, as shown by the way in which he has brought up his daughter Rebecca, a girl who has no secrets whatsoever from her father. However, Daniel's heart is in Zion; it throbs with love for his ancient homeland. He is not content to know that in times of trouble Jews of many lands tend to identify with their brethren in other countries; his ideal is the physical ingathering of all the Jews in Palestine.

Abraham Dreyfus[49] takes a somewhat derogatory view of Daniel. True, he does not deny that Dumas has good will toward the Jews, as shown by his very choice of the characters through whom he expresses his views on the Jewish race. "These characters," Dreyfus notes, "are Jews themselves, and the best one could find; they are Daniel, who proudly bears the name of the ancient prophet, and his daughter Rebecca, who is an angel." However, Dreyfus definitely feels that Dumas can hardly claim to have all of French Jewry on his side. The political and economic arguments which Daniel uses in preaching

---

[48]Alexandre Dumas, fils, *Femme de Claude*, Paris, 1873.
[49]A. Dreyfus, *op. cit.*

65

the emigration of the Jews to Palestine, Dreyfus says, are too weak. The quotation from the Passover Haggadah, "Next year in Jerusalem," which David cites at the end of the great oration in Act II, cannot be interpreted as the zealous idealist would have us understand it. When the Jews, at certain seasons, voice the prayerful wish, "Next year in Jerusalem," they are thinking of a purely spiritual Jerusalem, the Jerusalem of the Messianic era as foretold by the prophets; a time when all the nations of the world will put an end to hatred and war and unite to worship the One God. "The terrestrial site of that Jerusalem could even be Paris, if the nations, united in brotherhood, should agree to accept Paris as the capital of the Universe," he declares.

Considering himself a Frenchman through and through, Abraham Dreyfus reproaches Daniel with having forgotten that he is talking to French Jews. "For these Jews," he reminds him, "there is only one Fatherland, which has adopted them and which they love and defend. In all likelihood the itinerant visionary was not in France during the war [of 1871]."

Anatole Leroy-Beaulieu's[50] evaluation of Dumas' Daniel is a little more favorable. Lessing, he points out, has no monopoly on the portrayal of a Jewish paragon of virtue. As a matter of fact, Leroy-Beaulieu prefers Daniel of *La Femme de Claude* to Lessing's Nathan the Wise, "that verbose sophist with the frosty halo of wisdom." He describes Daniel as "an idealized Jewish type, much more true to life than the jackanapes of Paris would have thought a Jew to be. I have encountered this type myself—but far away from here, in the East [of Europe]. Alexandre Dumas' Daniel has become the progenitor of an entire generation; he seems to be the prototype of Mordecai, the latter-day prophet in *Daniel Deronda*."

Like Daniel in the drama by Dumas, Rachel, the Jewess in the novel *La Juive* (The Jewess),[51] by Enacryos* is in-

[50]*L'Espirit Juif* (The Jewish Spirit), from *Israël chez les Nations* (Israel Among the Nations) by Leroy-Beaulieu.
[51]Enacryos, *La Juive*, Paris, 1907.
*pseud. for J. H. Boex (1856–1940).

spired with a burning love for the land of her fathers. As a consequence of the Dreyfus affair, Zionism, the movement conceived by the Austrian journalist Theodor Herzl, has gained a foothold also in France, where it has given rise to the Zionist novel.

Born in the Alsatian village of Gruenhof as the daughter of a poor but honest man, Rachel grows up to become a dazzling beauty. She is also quite intelligent. She is just about to become engaged to a rabbi, when a French millionaire comes to Gruenhof, falls in love with her, and marries her. When Rachel, who speaks only a broken French, gets to Paris, she realizes that there are still many gaps in her education and doggedly sets about to make up for lost time. Before long, her husband, whom she never loved, dies, and Rachel is left a young widow living at the home of her father-in-law, Baruch.

She becomes an ardent Zionist after the death of her husband, and in her unrealistic fantasy she pictures the Jewish people already in possession of the Promised Land. Although she is not religious, she believes in the promise given in the Books of Genesis and Exodus.

However, Rachel is not only an ardent Zionist; she is also a passionate woman, made for love and for the struggle between the sexes. She suffers deeply because she cannot find any man among her own people who would satisfy her requirements for a husband. "The Middle Ages," she laments, cursing that era of persecution, "have broken the proud stature of the Jew." Eventually, strong and determined woman though she is, Rachel succumbs to her passion. She falls in love with Varades, a Gentile who condemns that which she holds most sacred—her love for her race—and wants to see the Jews merge with the peoples among whom they live. She becomes his mistress, whereupon her father-in-law tells her to marry her slightly anti-Semitic lover in order to save her honor. From now on, the old man says to her, she must utilize her strength for the task of raising her children to become good Jews.

Then disaster strikes. A rabid anti-Semite by the name

of Sully, who is convinced that the Jews will take over all of Europe, is in financial straits and comes to Baruch for help. When Baruch refuses aid to his mortal enemy because he first wants the satisfaction of seeing him grovel in his misery, Sully shoots and kills him. As a result, Rachel's sense of identification with her race reawakens and she sends her lover away.

Rachel's ideals are shared by her friend Picard. Picard, who has cast off the commercialism which, perhaps, attaches to the Jew by heredity, admires Rachel for her ardent loyalty to the Jewish race. He considers her beauty as proof that the Jews are not inferior to other races also in physical appearance. "The very survival of Judaism," Picard explains, "attests to the excellence of the race. While all the ancient civilizations have perished, the Jews have survived. Despite its close contacts with European civilization, Judaism has succeeded in preserving its unconquerable unity. The struggle between ancient Greece and Persia and that between the Roman Empire and the rest of the Ancient World are only minor episodes compared to the unflagging strength and staying power of the ancient tribe of Jacob."

Rachel and Picard, the two Zionists, are opposed by old Baruch and his friend Bernstamm. Since these two characters are introduced by the author as aids in his portrayal of Rachel and Picard, this study should include a brief sketch of them also.

Rachel's father-in-law Baruch, who describes himself as an ardent "Israelite," is opposed to Zionism because he considers it antediluvian nonsense. Notwithstanding his cynicism, he is a good man. He never shows compassion, but this definitely does not mean that he is incapable of love. He possesses a nimble mind and the famous—or notorious—Jewish versatility, taking a lively interest also in affairs outside his business pursuits. Arrogant and overweening, he must always have someone on whom he can bring his power to bear, an individual to whom he is superior and on whom he can force his ideas. Since he cherishes visions of justice

Baruch does not condemn the Socialists, but in his heart he regards them as interesting fools and a necessary evil.

Charles Bernstamm is one of the characters least objectionable to Rachel. He possesses tact and physical strength. However, he is given to fantastic ideas and to pessimism, and the active-minded Rachel particularly disapproves of his sluggishness. His father who, unlike his son, was a man of great vigor and energy, had him study science and philosophy. Thanks to his intelligence and his excellent memory he has acquired a wealth of knowledge and ideas. Believing that all things are alike, he is no more concerned about the fate of the Jews than he is about the future of the people of China.

Chapter 5:   The Jewess as a Woman of the World

Even if he is portrayed as a glowing idealist, it is generally accepted that the Jew in literature should be cast—at least
some of the time—as a comic character. As for the Jew in
drama, it is taken for granted that he must be a comic
figure.[52] The Jewish woman, by contrast, as we have already
shown, is almost always presented as a figure worthy of respect. "In this regard the poor Aryans frequently fall into the
trap," Anatole Leroy-Beaulieu notes.[53] "O happy Israel! His
salvation has ever come to him through a woman. Take the
novel; there, the Jewess, whether she be an angel of purity or
a strumpet, is always endowed with breathtaking beauty."
Chateaubriand,[54] too, noted the beauty of Jewish women and
gave a rather odd explanation for it. He points out that the
women of the Jewish race had no part in the sufferings and
humiliation of Christ; some Jewish women actually cheered
the Nazarene with a look of compassion and words of comfort.
As a reward, the women of the Jewish people were exempt
from the curse that had fallen on their menfolk. "A reflection
of the light of God has remained with them," the French
novelist says. Heinrich Heine's explanation for the unique
beauty of Jewish women seems more plausible. "The realization of the abject misery, the cruel disgrace and the myriad
dangers in which her friends and kinsmen live, has spread
upon her graceful features a sad expression of longing and of
sweet and alert anxiety that has a strange charm all its own."
But while Chateaubriand and Heine are very far apart indeed in their views, they agree that the physical pulchritude
of the Jewish woman is simply a reflection of her moral nobility. This is what makes the Jewish woman so interesting
as a heroine in the novel and in drama.

[52]Dumas, Preface to *La Femme de Claude.*
[53]Leroy-Beaulieu, *L'Esprit Juif* in *Israël chez les nations.*
[54]Cf. *Revue des Études Juives,* 1891. Lecture by Maurice Bloch: "The
Jewish Woman in German, English and French Fiction."

Maurice Bloch[55] discerns in her particularly those virtues which anti-Semites claim the Jewish race does not possess—frankness, altruism, nobility and courage. "Capable of any sacrifice, she occasionally rises to the heights of the sublime."

Many writers have portrayed Jewish women as courtesans; this comes as no great surprise, since the Jewess is supposed to typify beauty at its best. But even when she is cast in that role, the Jewess is shown in an appealing light and she remains a woman of virtue even in her vice.

Esther, the Jewess in Honoré Balzac's *Splendeurs et Misères des Courtisanes* (The Splendors and Miseries of Courtesans)[56] is a woman of charm and touching modesty. Her final letter to her sweetheart Lucien de Rubempré reveals true nobility of character.

"The soul may be sick, as the body is," she writes. "But the soul cannot submit stupidly to suffering like the body. . . . You gave me a whole life the day before yesterday, when you said that if Clotilde still refused you, you would marry me. It would have been a great misfortune for us both. . . . The world would never have accepted us. For two months I have been thinking of many things. . . . The world which grovels before money will not bow down before happiness or virtue—for I could have done good. Oh, how many tears I would have dried—as many as I have shed, I believe. Yes, I would have lived only for you and for charity."

The brothers Edmond (1822–1896) and Jules (1830–1870) Goncourt have also produced a Jewess who, although she belongs to the *demi-monde,* is on the whole a sympathetic character.

The Goncourts' novel *Manette Salomon,*[57] most of which depicts the life of artists in Paris, tells of a love affair between one such artist, Coriolis, and a Jewish girl, Manette Salomon. The characterization is very confusing and inconsistent; sometimes she is pictured in the brightest hues and then again she

[55]Cf. *Revue des Études Juives,* 1891. Bloch's lecture "The Jewish Woman in German, English and French Fiction."

[56]Balzac, *Splendeurs et Misères des Courtisanes,* Paris, 1843.

[57]Edmond and Jules de Goncourt, *Manette Salomon,* Paris, 1867.

is shown in the darkest colors. At first, we find her appealing
—at least to the extent that we can consider a courtesan to
be so. At the conclusion of the book, however, she is just another fallen woman for whose filthy vice the reader can feel
only contempt and disgust. Manette Salomon first meets Coriolis as a young girl. When he attempts to persuade her to pose
for him, she accepts the offer with alacrity. Soon Coriolis, en-
chanted with Manette's beauty, no longer looks at her with the
eye of an artist but with all the burning passion of which
Orientals such as he are capable. Taking stock of her situation,
Mannette figures she has nothing to lose by becoming the mistress of a noted artist.

Mannette Salomon is much like the other Jewish women
of Paris. She has cast off many of the Jewish traits which her
parents still had, and at first glance it would appear that she
has become completely assimilated into the Paris environment
in which she lives. But just as she has not been able to rid
herself of the external features of her race, so, too, she has not
succeeded in suppressing many of her other typically Jewish
traits. Although she has acquired many French characteristics
—her good-natured frivolity is typical of the Parisian woman—Manette is still very much a Jewess. She is also free of
the weaknesses of most women. Gold, precious stones, silks
and velvets, which hold so many charms for the average
woman, do not impress her. A member of "the race without
drunkards," she practices moderation in food and drink. In
fact, this strange girl dislikes amusements and diversions; her
notion of happiness is a quiet, uneventful life in a home to
which she is not bound by permanent ties. Having been
raised in surroundings where virtue was not preached day
after day, she sees nothing wrong in what she is doing.

Plagued by jealousy, Coriolis follows his mistress every-
where like a shadow. At first, Manette acts indifferent and
regards him as nothing more than an employer. In time, however, she begins to reciprocate her simple and good-natured
lover's affection, and when Coriolis scores a resounding success in his work, she falls passionately in love with him. Still,
she acts as innocent as a child and even turns out to be a girl

of fine character; when her lover becomes ill, she keeps constant watch at his bedside like any woman who is determined to keep her man alive. The young Jewess comes to mean more and more to the artist; he finds himself falling deeply in love with Manette, who seems to be innocent of all lust for power. However, there is a gradual, subtle but very definite change in Manette's role in the artist's household. The attractive young woman begins to show masculine personality traits while her lover becomes increasingly effeminate. When Manette has a baby, she changes beyond recognition. Cold tenacity, stubbornness and greed seem to have sown their evil seeds in her blood. She talks and dreams only about the wealth which she wants first for herself and secondly to pass on to her child. The idol to which she now clings with every fiber of her being is the mighty Mammon. On the face of it, one might think that she has suddenly turned religious, for she returns to the faith and to the customs of her ancestors. Before long, however, we find out that she is not motivated by religious feeling but by crude selfishness. She wants to win the God of the Jews as her ally so that He will help her get the riches she longs for.

Coriolis, effete and spent, bows to her tyranny. He is forced to abandon his life's ideal—the pursuit of art for art's sake. Harassed and tormented by Manette, he now paints only to earn quick money. He has sacrificed his art to the idol of his mistress. He is no longer an artist but a hired hand.

In substance, the novel *Mademoiselle Fifi,* by Guy de Maupassant (1850–1893),[58] bears some resemblance to the Goncourts' *Manette Salomon.* However, Maupassant's Jewess, Rachel, though she is no less immoral than Manette, has some virtues; she is brave and she is patriotic. In fact, she eventually musters sufficient strength and energy to turn over a new leaf. "Mademoiselle Fifi" is the nickname of a Prussian officer billeted in a castle near Rouen during the Franco-Prussian war. To kill time, he and his brother officers have ladies of easy virtue brought to the castle. Altogether, five French girls turn up. There is much feasting and even more drinking. Fifi

[58]Guy de Maupassant, *Mademoiselle Fifi,* Paris, 1886.

gets drunk, he calls for three cheers for the Prussian army, and then proceeds to mock the defeats of the French and to insult France. Of the five French girls, four, outraged though they are, make no move to stop him. Not so Rachel, the Jewess. Furious, she leaps to her feet, mortally wounds the officer and then escapes through a window. An entire Prussian batallion is sent after her in hot pursuit, but Rachel eludes them. The priest of the parish allows her to hide out in the belfry of his church.

Asked to conduct funeral services for the dead officer, the priest has the bells of his church toll for the first time since France has gone into mourning for her defeat. He has to do it, for otherwise the Prussian soldiers would seize the church, go up into the belfry themselves and discover Rachel there. Thus, by acceding to the Prussian command, the priest saves the Jewish girl from capture. After the war Rachel marries a good, tolerant man and the two live happily ever after.

Chapter 6: The Jewish Family

A striking contrast to the Jewish women discussed in the preceding chapter is represented by Sorle in Erckmann-Chatrian's novel *Le Blocus de Phalsbourg*[59] (The Blockade of Pfalzburg). Sorle, the wife of Moyse, is a respectable matron, an excellent cook and housekeeper, and a devoted wife and mother. She is loved by everyone who knows her, including Sergeant Trubert, a formidable old soldier and veteran of the Napoleonic wars, who is now stationed at Pfalzburg. Trubert does not like the Jews; he does not have good memories of those with whom he happened to have dealings in Russia and Poland. When he is first informed at the mayor's office that he will be billeted with a Jewish family, the sergeant is furious. "They're sending me to some Jews," he mutters. "They'd better watch out or I'll smash everything." However, Trubert has reckoned without his host, or rather without his Jewish hostess, who gives him a cordial welcome and delicious meals. Try as he may, the short-tempered sergeant, the terror of all the families with whom he has been billeted in the past, can find no fault with his Jewish hosts. There is nothing for him to curse about; the house is immaculate. Surprised and delighted, he shakes hands with every member of the family and then says to Moyse: "Well, Papa Moyse, you can be proud of that fine wife of yours. Now that's what I call a woman." The longer he is with them, the more the sergeant grows to like the Jewish family. One day, during the siege, he brings his own scanty meat ration which he got from the barracks and gives it to the children of his host, who are sick with typhoid fever. Sorle is deeply touched at this gesture because she had no meat in the house and needed meat desperately to make broth for her sick children. Trubert is happy to be able to help these Jews, who have become his friends. When the siege is over and he is transferred, he parts from his host with genuine

[59]Erckmann-Chatrian, *Le Blocus de Phalsbourg*, Paris, 1867.

75

regret. Before leaving, he asks permission to embrace Madame Sorle.

"Yes," Maurice Bloch comments, "Sorle, this good, fine woman, whose whole life has been one of honor, work and godliness, who has raised her children and has been a loyal helpmate to her husband typifies the woman [of valor] whose praises are sung by the Proverbs of Solomon in the Bible."[60]

Sorle's husband, Moyse, has somewhat provincial views. He fails to appreciate the bold policies and military genius of Napoleon; he sees him only as a ruthless tyrant who will stop at nothing to attain his ends. He is sickened by the thought that thousands of innocent people should be sacrificed to the ambitions of one man. Moyse has still retained some of the ways of the ghetto and is the laughing-stock of his comrades in the National Guard. But Moyse is much more humane than most of the soldiery which has become bestialized by constant warfare. When a young deserter, a simple-minded fellow who did not realize the seriousness of his act, is sentenced to death, Moyse finds that many of his fellow-soldiers are actually looking forward to watching the execution. He feels he is partly to blame for the death of the lovesick youth because it was he, Moyse, who first reported him absent without leave. He leaves no stone unturned to move the military judges to have pity on the boy and eventually succeeds in getting the deserter acquitted.

Moyse would gladly have sacrificed his own life if by so doing he could have saved the life of his sick grandson. The mother of the little boy, unable to bear the loss of her child, dies soon after him. The family fears also for Moyse at the moment when the sexton of the synagogue makes a rent in the grandfather's coat as a sign of mourning. Again and again the old man kisses the cold body of the child, which is dressed in a tiny shirt and holds a *tallith*[61] in his hand. Moyse is sustained only by his deep faith in God; in due time, he

---

[60]*Revue des Études Juives*. Maurice Bloch's lecture, "The Jewish Woman in German, English and French Fiction."

[61]Prayer shawl.

can even feel happy and contented again as he sees his work carried on by his three able sons.

Alexandre Weil's novel *Couronne*[62] is a veritable hymn of praise to Jewish womanhood. Coronne, a charming Alsatian girl, is the daughter of well-to-do parents. Her father, M. Riche, is a businessman who has very little time for his family because he is working hard in order to be able to give his daughters generous doweries when they marry. Mme Riche is a fine woman, who needs affection and is not free of the weaknesses of small-town people. For instance, she thinks her daughter is crazy to cry over the book *Paul et Virginie*. Mme Riche saves all her tears for Tisha B'Av, the fast day commemorating the destruction of Jerusalem. Couronne has much to commend her. Beautiful without being conscious of it, she is serious and mature, and considers it more important to help with the housework or to do a neighbor a good turn than to deck herself out in fine clothes like her sister Eva.

Couronne's parents have a boarder, a Jewish village schoolteacher by the name of Elias Seibel. He has no money, but he is a highly educated young man. One fine day Elias loses his position. Only now does Couronne realize that she loves him; before that time she was not aware of her instinctive desire to be in the company of the young man and to let him know with a look that she enjoys being with him. She loves the sick schoolteacher because he is educated and as fine a person as she herself is. She scorns the attentions of the wealthy young men in her village who have acquired a thin veneer of smoothness to cover up their coarseness and who try to cloak their lack of education and refinement with flowery turns of phrase. Couronne is happy without knowing it; it is a pure and innocent happiness. In her naiveté she thinks she will be able to nurture this love in her heart indefinitely without ever making it known. But when she learns of Seibel's dismissal she begins to pine away with lover's grief. Elias, the victim of vicious slander, goes off to Algeria with hardly a cent to his name.

Alexandre Weil gives a vivid and appealing description

[62]Alexandre Weil, *Couronne*, Paris, 1868.

of the Passover Seder at the Riche home. Everyone is in a gay holiday mood except for Couronne, who sits quietly at the table, pale and sad. Worried about her daughter. Mme Riche calls the doctor, who tries various medicines. But Couronne grows weaker by the day, and her mother spends entire nights at her bedside, weeping to see "this flower which faded and might well perish." One night, the wise mother asks the girl: "Couronne, if I were to ask M. Elias to come back, after the insulting letter I wrote him, do you think he would come back to us?" In reply, Couronne throws her arms around her mother and cries out: "Mama, he'd come back even if he were Emperor." But Elias is no longer an impecunious schoolteacher. He is secretary and confidant to the Governor of Algeria and has become an influential figure in public life. There is talk in the village that Elias could have his pick of the wealthiest girls in the land and would never marry a poor village girl like Couronne. Particularly one of the village matrons, Madame Feissel, goes about making bets that this fine gentleman will never stray into Alsace again. But Elias fools them all; he returns to a joyous reunion with Couronne. Now that her sweetheart has returned, Couronne makes a quick recovery, her parents gladly give their consent to the marriage and Couronne happily goes off to Algiers with her husband.

"Alexandre Weil shows us graceful young girls, Jewish women who are devoted to their families, who have respect for sacred traditions and are themselves deserving of universal appreciation and respect," Maurice Bloch states. "Like Erckmann-Chatrian, Alexandre Weil likes to portray good people who enjoy helping their neighbors and, better still, are eager to serve their happiness without ulterior motives. Alexandre Weil is a fine complement to Erckmann-Chatrian. . . .

"Alexandre Weil wants to do more than merely tell a story and entertain his readers; he wants to teach them, and sometimes he imparts important moral lessons. He shows that the best marriages are not money marriages. Parents who are not mindful of hearts but consider only money and position frequently bring cruel disappointments and bitter remorse upon themselves as well as upon their children. Beauty is not the sole feminine virtue; in the eyes of Alexandre Weil, in fact, it may well be the least important. The virtue he seeks in women above all else is moral beauty; he looks for qualities of the heart and of the soul."[63]

Georges Stenne's* novel *Perles*[64] is closely patterned on Weil's novel. Here too, the setting is a village in the Alsace. The theme is the same in both novels, and the characters bear a striking resemblance to each other.

M. Roos is a stodgy villager who is not easily put out; his wife is gossipy, but a good housekeeper and mother. Their daughter, Leah, is the counterpart of Couronne's sister, Eva. She is on good terms with all the young men in her home town, trying to keep them all on the string so she can make her choice among the wealthiest of the lot when she is ready to settle down. She even manages to ensure a simple and vain little schoolmaster, Emanuel, who is the counterpart of Elias Seibel in *Couronne*. Leah's sister Perles is an unassuming, sensitive and intelligent girl and, like Weil's Couronne, she plays something of a Cinderella role in her family. Perles, too, falls in love with a schoolteacher (Emanuel), who reciprocates her affection but, like Elias and Couronne, Emanuel and Perles, too, are not aware of their love for each other. Again like Couronne, Perles goes into a decline for the love of Emanuel, but in the case of Perles, the doctor, instead of trying out medicines, makes the correct diagnosis at once and gets in touch with his friend Emanuel, who has gone away on a long trip in an effort to get over a bad case of lover's grief. Overjoyed, Emanuel returns home and marries Perles.

Perles presents one character who has no counterpart in Weil's *Couronne;* namely, Rabbi Loeb. Like M. Riche in Weil's novel, Stenne's M. Roos has remained faithful to traditional Judaism, but in both cases, this attachment is lukewarm and based more on force of habit than on true conviction. Rabbi Loeb, by contrast, is definitely an Orthodox

[63]Lecture by Maurice Bloch on Alexandre Weil, Paris, 1903.

[64]Georges Stenne, *Perles,* Paris, 1871.

*Pseudonym of David Schornstein (1826–79).

Jew, the type who has remained untouched by secular education and has declared uncompromising war on everything modern.

Georges Stenne has depicted a splendid Jewish woman also in his short story *La Dîme* (The Tithe).[65] Noémie, the daughter of an impecunious Torah scribe and cantor, musters all the will power and self-restraint at her command to repress her feelings for the man she loves because she knows that the relationship would cause her parents distress. Her heart is torn between love and filial duty, and her sense of duty wins out. As a matter of fact, she is ready to marry a man she does not love so that she can assist her parents financially.

The whole story is one hymn of praise to Jewish family life; even those characters who are not appealing in other respects are willing to make any sacrifice that may be required of them for the welfare of their family.

Rebecca in Dumas'[66] *La Femme de Claude* is piety personified. In this play Dumas sounds an alarm, calling on his audience to remember the tragic lessons of the Franco-Prussian War of 1870. He wants to remind his countrymen that God, country, work, honor, love, marriage, motherhood, and childhood are all sacred concepts to be taken seriously. In his Prologue to *La Femme de Claude* Dumas asserts that while Corneille's *Le Cid* is a great work of art, it does not have the same significance seen from the moral point of view. Chimène should not have married Rodrigo; there are situations, Dumas says, when a woman should be willing to sacrifice her happiness because she loves virtue more.

In view of the above, Maurice Bloch[67] considers it most flattering to the Jews that a drama with such lofty moral purposes should feature a Jewish woman as a character worthy of emulation. Claude is in love with Rebecca, a Jewish girl, who reciprocates his affection. The trouble is that Claude is already married to a woman whose entire character is in sharp contrast to that of Rebecca. Rebecca leaves Claude;

[65]Georges Stenne, *La Dîme,* Paris, 1873.
[66]Dumas, fils, *La Femme de Claude,* Paris, 1873.
[67]Cf. *Revue des Études Juives,* 1891. Bloch's lecture, "The Jewish Woman in German, English and French Fiction."

"she sacrifices herself in her youth, in her beauty." At the same times the Jewish girl is cast in the role of a prophetess; she is made to proclaim to mankind that there is something infinitely greater than our own petty concerns, beyond the limits of earthly existence. Rebecca throws herself into the spheres of the infinite, finding strength and consolation outside this world. Her farewell to Claude, who cannot marry her, reveals her high ideals but would seem more appropriate coming from a nun who has turned her back on the world than from a Jewish woman who accepts life:

"When death shall have freed us," she says to him, "you from the bonds, me from terrestrial submissions, you will find me, a patient and unmaterial bride, awaiting you on the threshold of the unknown and we shall be united in the Infinite. . . . I am the bride of the second life." As a contrast to this pure Jewish maiden, Dumas presents Césarine, an adulteress who does not recoil from crime, including treason.

Even Bourget's novel *Cosmopolis,* which features Justus Hafner, a repulsive Jewish huckster, idealizes Jewish womanhood in the person of Hafner's daughter Fanny, who is portrayed as a veritable angel. Her physical appearance alone attests to the ideal type of the Semitic beauty. In addition, she is deeply religious. But her father, whose religion has always been commingled with local concerns, the affairs of his home town, and everyday politics, has no time to teach his child to love her ancestral faith.

In Fanny's home wealth is worshipped as the sole ideal worth aspiring after. Fanny has to adopt the Protestant faith because her father considers it the expedient thing to do. However, after the death of her mother, Fanny comes under the influence of a Catholic woman, and since the true medium or religious education among the unlearned is neither doctrine nor conviction but environment, the devout Catholic woman quickly gains control over the thoughts of her irresolute Judeo-Protestant friend. From that time on Fanny has her heart set on being accepted into the bosom of her friend's Church because she wants to go to heaven when she dies.

However, her father, Justus Hafner, says that she must make her religious affiliation dependent on that of the man she will marry. In the end she marries a Catholic by the name of Ardea. It is a forced marriage and makes her unhappy, but it also brings her a fine friendship with Alba, a noble-woman who has suffered the same fate as she. It is to Alba that Fanny pours out her heart, because her father would not understand. Nevertheless, Fanny loves her father and, in fact, regards him as a saint.

"While she may have become a Protestant or a Catholic, Fanny is of Jewish descent. Thus, she comes of an oppressed race which, in addition to the less desirable traits typical of all victims of persecution, has inevitably developed also the virtues characteristic of a people in that position—family pride, selflessness and, in the case of women, utter self-denial. The Jewish woman thinks of herself as the jewel of her constantly threatened home, as the flower that spreads its fragrance through the dark prison in which she is confined. This explains Fanny's affection for her father. For the same reason, it is only natural that she should be pious."

Side by side with the upstart Ephraim Monach, Robert de Bonnières,[68] too, features an attractive female character. Even Monach's mother elicits a measure of admiration. But more than the old woman, Lia, the baron's daughter, is every bit as charming as all the other Jewish women in French drama and in the French novel.

Everyone who meets her is captivated by the impression of wholesome vigor and energy she conveys. Her father has gradually weaned her away from the influence of her pious grandmother because he feels that Lia should be free to choose her own religion when she grows up. By the time she is thirteen, Lia is a real woman. At first, her Gentile classmates marvel at her precocious beauty, but eventually they become jealous of her, and their envy only serves to aggravate the dislike they had for the little intruder from the very outset. Mme Monach, on the whole, is the antitype of her husband, though she moves a little more gracefully than he amidst the

[68]See pp. 29–30 above.

luxuries they have acquired. She urges her daughter to cultivate the friendship of the Gentile girls, no matter what the cost. Lia makes every effort to follow her mother's advice and repays insults with courtesy to get herself into the good graces of the girls. But one day she comes home in tears and tells her mother, "I can't go on—they simply do not want to love me." However, as her classmates grow older, they become more mature and discerning, and eventually they treat the wealthy and beautiful Lia with the respect which the world as a rule accords to the very rich.

Roger, the general's son, admires Lia not only for her beauty, but also for her good sense, her charm, her intelligence, and last but by no means least, for her ambition. She feels that she will not be able to develop her skills and charms to full potential as long as she remains Jewish. She is determined to break the shackles that hold her back and to become a Christian so that she may be able to mingle with the rest of the world and shine forth in all her brilliance.

She has sufficient will power to get over her unhappy love affair. Her father then tries to arrange a match for her with another Gentile baron. But now she spurns every proposal of marriage with contempt and disgust.

In this connection, we refer the reader to Anatole France's *L'Orme du Mail*,[69] which we have discussed earlier in this study.

Worms-Clavelin, the Jewish prefect, admires and respects his wife Noémie for her ability to impress even anti-Semitic Gentiles, who enjoy her company. The fashionable set does not consider her particularly intelligent, but they regard her as an honest, gentle and good woman. Noémie is modest and reserved when she is in company—she shows approval and admiration for what she sees, but she does not talk much.

In France's novel *Le Mannequin d'Osier*[70] (*Histoire Contemporaine*, Part II) (The Willow Mannequin) Noémie appears in a less favorable light beside her daughter Jeanne.

[69]See pp. 14 and 15 above.

[70]A. France, *Le Mannequin d'Osier*, Paris, 1896.

Instead of supervising her daughter's education herself, Noémie has had the girl baptized and has sent her to an exclusive convent school where she is to acquire those accomplishments which will later help her make a brilliant match. Madame Worms-Clavelin is one of the pillars of the Catholic Church in France and a leader in many Catholic charitable organizations.

In contrast to her luxury-loving mother, Jeanne is simple and unassuming. She loves and admires her father, of whose outstanding abilities she has heard much from the Sisters at the convent school. She has less respect for her mother. The relationship between mother and daughter can best be judged from the following characterization given by Jeanne herself. "Mother," she says, "Some people like linen, others like dresses, and some like jewelry. You, Mother, are fond of jewelry. Me, I like linen."*

In a very modern novel, *L'Opprobre* (The Disgrace),[71] Albert Compain depicts a Jewish woman who can be considered likeable at least in comparison with her Gentile lady friends.

Gustav Ledermann is a wealthy Jew and an honest businessman. His wife is a simple but good-natured woman. For quite some time her feelings toward her husband have been nothing more than friendship, but she enjoys conjuring up shadows of long-departed love by playing matchmaker, arranging marriages in keeping with the bourgeois conventions she cherishes. One of the girls whom she wants to marry off is Thérèse, a young lady who has no parents and who gives art lessons to a group of young girls meeting regularly at the Ledermann home. Noting how sad the girl looks and acts, Madame Ledermann thinks it is high time Thérèse got married. When Thérèse's grandmother dies, Madame Ledermann all but adopts the girl and invites her to live at her home. But much as she loves Madame Ledermann, Thérèse cannot accept the offer. She has fallen in love with a young

---

*The girl implies that her mother is more careful about her outer clothing than about what she wears beneath.

[71]Albert Compain, *L'Opprobre,* Paris, 1905.

law student, but he has left her to marry a girl with a substantial dowry. Thérèse considers it her duty to tell Madame Ledermann the truth about the sad situation in which she now finds herself. She is sure that this lady, who has always been so kind to her, will give her help and sympathy. Instead, Madame Ledermann reproaches her for having fallen for such an unscrupulous climber and advises her to give up her baby so that people will not know about it and she will not suffer disgrace. Despite Madame Ledermann's repeated warnings about the perils of defying convention and violating the sensibilities of society, Thérèse is determined to endure the consequences of her illicit relationship and to raise her baby herself. Out of pity for the expectant mother, Madame Ledermann allows her to go on teaching her daughter for the time being, and keeps the girl's secret to herself. When the baby comes, Thérèse keeps it out of sight, but people "find out" just the same and before long the art teacher's disgrace has become the talk of the town. Fearing for the innocence of their daughters, the parents of the girls in the art class decide to discontinue the lessons. In the end Madame Ledermann, too, breaks down and gives "propriety" its due. Sadly, she sits down and writes a letter to Thérèse in which she encloses some money and asks her not to come to her home again.

CONCLUSION

Looking over the novels and dramas discussed in this study, we note that many of the Jewish characters have German or "Jewish" surnames[72] like Gundermann, Ephraim Monach, Rakowitz, Mrs. Langmann, Showten, Horn, Voewenberg, Hendelsohn, Strohmann, Nathan, Schleifmann, Baruch, Bernstamm and Ledermann. Many of them, like Rachel and Baruch in Enacryos' *La Juive,* have come to France from Alsace-Lorraine. Others, like Gundermann in Zola's *L'Argent,* Bonnière's family Monach, Bourget's Justus Hafner, Mme Langmann and Showten in Charnaicé's *Baron Vampire,* Horn in Lavedan's *Prince d'Aurec,* Voewenberg, Hendelsohn and Dr. Lurdau in Donnay's *Retour de Jérusalem,* Strohmann and Nathan in Guinon's *Décadence,* the Blochs in Nozière's *Baptême,* Schleifmann in Vandérem's *Les Deux Rives,* and the Ledermanns in Compain's *L'Opprobre* are German Jews. Others again, like Balzac's *Gobsec,* are of Belgian or Dutch origin, while Bourget's Crémieux-Dax and De Vogüé's Bayonne are of Spanish descent.

Some of the stories, such as *L'Ami Fritz, Le Blocus de Phalsbourg, Couronne, Perles* and *La Dîme,* are set in Alsace or in Lorraine.

Since this is by no means an isolated phenomenon, one wonders whether these authors have a specific reason for portraying their Jewish characters as quasi-foreigners. Anti-Semitic authors might be expected to follow this trend because it is their way of repudiating the Jews, but it seems that even philo-Semitic literature depicts at least some of its Jewish figures as alien elements in France.

The differences in the treatment the various authors accord to the Jews in their writings can be explained quite

[72]Guinon has his Jewish characters use German expressions. Many of the Jews in Mme. de Gyp's writings have German accents.

easily in terms of the views and philosophies each writer represents. It stands to reason that Bourget, who is a nationalist and something of an anti-Semite, will not have the same approach to Jews as Zola,[73] the democrat who preaches the brotherhood of all mankind. Nor can Guinon, the gutter anti-Semite, be expected to see the Jews in the same light as Erckmann and Chatrian, who numbered the rabbi of their home town among their closest friends.

Just as in everyday life the pessimist tends to see only the dark side of his fellowmen, while the optimist seeks to discover the good in humanity, so in literature, anti-Semitic writers, whether they are aware of it or not, emphasize the flaws in the character of the Jew, while the authors who favor the Jews point out and glorify the noble traits they see in their Jewish subjects.

Of the various Jewish character types found in French literature of centuries past all are cast exclusively as money men.[74] But the Jew of nineteenth-century literature is no longer the small-time peddler he was in the eighteenth century; today he appears as the big banker who reigns supreme on the money market. The Jew in the role of a loyal patriot, a skilled statesman, a Socialist or a Zionist does not make his first appearance until the nineteenth century.

Nineteenth-century literature also reflects a certain trend within Judaism[75] although, like all other developments, this tendency, too, is curbed from time to time by various factors. The Jew who, during the first half of the nineteenth century and even beyond the 1850's, remained firmly rooted in the traditional Judaism of his ancestors, is later shown as becoming increasingly assimilated into the French environment in which he lives. In order to make life easier for himself and not to shut himself off from chances for a brilliant future, he throws his ancestral faith overboard like so much ballast

---

[73]Zola juxtaposes Gundermann and the Gentile Saccard, compared to whom the Jew may almost be said to appear in a favorable light.

[74]French literature has no counterpart to *Nathan the Wise*.

[75]Cf. Author's preface.

and either remains indifferent to religion or converts to Christianity.

Due to the victory of the Republican bloc over the Center and the Nationalists, atheism had become the credo of the French people, a philosophy which has been worshipped as the "answer to everything" once before; that is, during the Age of Enlightenment. It is only natural that the irreligion of the majority of the people of France should have promoted assimilation among the Jews, a process which may well be completed unless liberalism should be supplanted by reaction. More recently, however, anti-Semitic authors have adopted a new approach; namely, that of racial anti-Semitism, which sees the Jew not as an alien in name only, but as a foreign body within the corpus of the French people. This new trend and its influence on French public opinion may well work to delay the assimilation of French Jewry.